DIARY OF A FOOD ADDICT

Herbert Greene
Carolyn Jones

DIARY OF A
FOOD ADDICT

GROSSET & DUNLAP
PUBLISHERS, New York

To those whose reach is still
imprisoned by their grasp—
And to those who try to set them free.

DIARY OF A FOOD ADDICT

was not burdened with eyes or ears. The air was filled with vibrant fragrances: voices floated on scented currents into my nose.

"How long has he been out?"

"About six hours. He'll come around any time now."

"How bad is it?"

"It's all on the chart."

"Christ! This guy's a mess. A couple of busted ribs, fractures in both legs, multiple lacerations . . ."

"I wonder what he'll say when you tell him?"

"When I tell him what?"

I was curious too. Who were they talking about? My eyes drifted snugly back into place, but remained pleasantly shut.

"Charlie, you're gonna die laughing when I tell you. This guy was standing on the island divider on Park Avenue. A cab clipped him and knocked him into the opposite lane, where he got hit again. A patrol car happened to be there and the cops saw the whole thing. It was all this guy's fault."

"Come on, Willie. If he was on the divider and the cab didn't jump the curb, how could he get hit in the first place?"

I smiled at this absurdity. But my mouth didn't move.

"That's the funny part. Look at this guy, Charlie. He's about a hundred pounds overweight. The over-hang of his gut is about nine inches. So when the cab shaved the curb kind of close, the side-view mirror caught a piece of him."

"What's so funny about that? Man, I hate these fat slobs. They make a joke out of medicine. What a case to finish off my residency with!"

"Charlie, where's your sense of humor?"

I vainly struggled to open my mouth, to tell Charlie how funny a sense of humor is, and maybe he shouldn't be so hard on that fat guy.

"Willie, what the hell am I supposed to do when he has to start walking? The minute he puts his weight on those healed fractures he'll bust them wide open."

"Relax, Charlie. You got him where you want him. He's not going anyplace. You can start melting the fat off him right away."

"What if he won't cooperate? Do you realize that because of this ox, my last year of residency could be at stake?"

"He's got a little something at stake too, Charlie. If he doesn't get that lard off, he could spend the rest of his life in a wheelchair."

"What difference would that make to him? Look at

him. How much time do you think he spends off his duff and on his feet anyway?"

"Plenty. He's one of the top conductors on Broadway. He's conducted some of the biggest hits ever. *Guys and Dolls, Silk Stockings, The Most Happy Fella.* He even won a Tony for *The Music Man.* Name's Herb Greene."

Herb Greene?

That's me!

They're talking about me!!

Now I fought to keep my eyes shut, to keep from moving, to keep from being noticed.

When the doctors left, I felt as if I'd been hit by lightning. The shock of being smashed up was bad enough. Learning that my obesity was responsible was even more shattering. But the fact that my recovery depended upon my losing weight, something I'd found impossible to do all my life, left me hopeless.

I'll never make it, I thought. Never. That cab should have finished me off.

Why can't a New York taxi driver do anything right?

Somehow, I lived through my self-pity. Although the many months that followed could hardly be called living, except in the technical sense. The boredom of confinement, the torment of itchy casts, the humiliation of my total dependency upon the nurses and doctors were miserable enough, but crowning everything was my daily diet of three cups of bouillon: a combination sufficient to satisfy the ambitions of any serious martyr.

And the dreams I endured every night! Food. Tables of food, sometimes even mountains of food. I would look at it, circle it, smell it, but never taste a morsel.

One morning, after a particularly trying dream, a laboratory technician rolled in his cart of test tubes, finger-puncture gadgets and his infinite variety of blood-sucking devices.

"Good morning, Mr. Greene," he said cheerfully,

"we need a couple of blood samples. You know, for the lab Dracula."

I nodded, still floating on an enormous cloud of whipped cream. The sharp prick in my index finger curdled the cream. As the technician inhaled my drop of blood through a narrow plastic tube, the door opened. and three smiling nurses entered. One was carrying a huge box wrapped in plain brown paper.

"Well, well, Mr. Greene. You have a package from your friend Max Erlanger."

"I don't know any Max Erlanger, nurse. Sorry, wrong number," I said and winced as the lab guy stuck a monster into my arm.

"No mistake about it. The man delivered it himself just to be sure. There's a card with it."

"It's got to be a mistake," I said.

She shook her head stubbornly, her face set in that nurse expression that's exactly the same whether celebrating an enema or administering a birthday. I accepted there had been no mistake.

"Nurse, would you please read it?"

While nurse number one held on to an obviously heavy load, number two opened an envelope and read haltingly:

Dear Mr. Greene:

I just got back from the Hack Bureau. Me and my partner. They're particular down there and it took weeks before they got satisfied about your accident.

It was your letter. The one where you said the whole thing was your fault. Boy, your accident, which you admitted was your fault, was a big break for me be-cause they didn't take away our license.

As tokens of both our esteems, my partner and me want you to have this and enjoy life a little in a lousy hospital room.

Yours truly,
Max Erlanger and Partner Jim Roza

Number two replaced the letter in the envelope. Number one cleared her throat.

"That was a very generous thing you did for them, Mr. Greene," she said.

I shrugged and thought that if I had been a few inches less generous to my belly, none of this would have happened.

"Would you like us to open it for you?"

"Please."

The three showed their training and teamwork as they skillfully cut and peeled off the cover in no time, revealing a white box with gold lettering:

TWENTY-FIVE POUNDS OF THE
WORLD'S FINEST CHOCOLATES

The nurses looked at the candy, looked at one an-other in horror and very suspiciously turned their eyes on me. Before I could deny collusion, they marched out in unison, candy box secured.

But there was a brighter side to this episode. From that time on, I never had another dream about food.

Throughout my stay in the hospital, I was unusually

cooperative, calm and even cheerful. Sometimes downright elated. Because secretly, I believed the punishment fit my crime. On the rare occasions I groused, it was over a change in routine. The biggest such change was brought about by the appearance of George, my physiotherapist. He was treated with great respect by the doctors and nurses, who claimed he had an instinctive genius for his calling.

I grew to dislike George. There was something about his constant preoccupation with arms, legs, muscles and such that I found unappealing. Dark, short, hirsute, with a trace of accent I never could identify, he was a deceptively powerful man. Many times he would catch my falling body and carry me effortlessly around and around the physiotherapy room, patiently explaining that no matter how upset I became, how much agony the therapy caused me, my complaints wouldn't have the slightest effect upon the tissues of my legs and flabby abdominal muscles. Then he would plunk me down between the parallel bars and the therapy would continue.

One day, after a particularly frustrating battle to keep myself upright, George called time out. I was relieved because I knew for sure I'd never run the four-minute mile, and also I was pretty tired. While I rested, George busied himself with a new contraption he had dreamed up for a special group of patients he had scheduled after my Olympic exhibition.

"Say, Mr. Greene," he said, as he monkeyed with his nuts and bolts, "I hear you lead lots of orchestras in your business. That right?"

"No more than you can shake a stick at."

"That's a good one," he said, but his delivery implied that another good one like that and he wouldn't bother to catch me the next time I stumbled.

"So it's a lousy one," I admitted.

"Yeah," he agreed, "lousy."

"Why do you ask?"

"Sometimes I wonder about things like this and that."

"Wonder about what, George?"

"Oh, sometimes I wonder if you become orchestra leader because you don't play the violin so good."

It was an old joke and a chance for a return shot.

"That's a good one," I replied, mimicking him.

"No, that's a lousy one," he flatly corrected me.

"Well, I play the violin very lousy too. In fact, I don't play the violin. I play the piano."

"Say, that's right," he said altogether too brightly, "so how's about some music?"

Before I could think of an answer, George was bounding gracefully across the therapy room. Reaching the far end, he pulled the cover off a spinet, rolled it across the floor and brought it to a stop in front of me.

"Now let's see if you lead orchestras because you don't play the piano either."

I looked at the little Steinway and felt stark terror. I didn't think I had enough strength to use the pedals. My hands felt stiff and tired from doing my leg work on the parallel bars in addition to whatever hands do anyway. All in all, I was not well prepared for this kind of thing, considering how long it had been since I had last made music.

"What you waiting for, Mr. Greene, Carnegie Hall?" George sang out challengingly.

"Not exactly Carnegie Hall, George," I stalled, but I was fast running short of stiff upper lip. "I need some inspiration. You know, an audience. I just can't play for a bunch of exercise machines."

The instant the words left my mouth, I wished they hadn't. Bravado was one thing, but I had no business hurting George's feelings. Before I could apologize, George was off and running.

"You got a big heart, Mr. Greene," he shouted over his shoulder, "so I'll fix you up."

He opened the entrance door with a flourish. A group of smiling nurses wheeled in the patients scheduled to try out George's newest therapeutic device: a gaggle of kids and an old man, accompanied by my personal doctor, Frank Brooks, chief of orthopedics.

I felt the same old fluttering butterflies that never failed to do their stuff every opening night I ever conducted. So, I took my usual opening night gulp of air and plunged into a medley of songs from a bunch of those opening nights. Nobody seemed to mind the clinkers I hit, nor did anybody appear to miss the pedals I was too shaky to step on. After fifteen minutes or so, when I wound up pounding the piano like drums for "76 Trombones," George decided it was enough for a first time. As though my panting and sweating didn't clue him that for an encore I'd faint. But the cheered-up faces I saw cheered me up much more in return.

As George wheeled me back to my room, he said, "That's pretty good, Mr. Greene. But you sure are lucky you got that conducting trade up your sleeve."

Whatever he had up his sleeve, however, had little to do with music. He simply made therapeutic use of the piano by the old carrot and stick game as my strength returned. If I wanted to play it, I had to move it. He said it was great for the hamstrings and back muscles.

Although I never learned to love George, I did learn, through him, to respect and even enjoy my own body. While he wasn't sympathetic, he was never cruel and never failed to encourage a hard effort, a show of progress or the tiniest growth of my determination not to cave in. What George gave to me, beyond a literal acceptance of living in the sweat of my brow, was the knowledge that change was not necessarily married to catastrophe.

I began to see that the change brought about in my life by my accident might be for the best, when all was said and done.

Although I had made many attempts, I had never been able to stay on a reducing diet on my own, at least not long enough to make any lasting difference. But now, I was no longer alone: I was surrounded by people who cared, people who would, if necessary, viciously starve off every spare ounce of my flesh in order to help me.

I had a growing belief that once all the extra weight was gone, when I'd look and feel like everybody else, the change itself would insure that the weight would never come back. And whenever I thought of Max Erlanger, the cab driver who shaved that curb a bit close, I not only forgave him, but wished him long life, many flag drops and immunity from mugging.

Six months later I left the hospital completely recovered and in excellent shape for the first time in my adult life. And positively svelte minus one hundred pounds.

But I had become so involved in healing my bones and remaking my flesh that it never occurred to me to wonder how my life would be changed by all that health.

When I realized that the true test of my courage wasn't behind me in the hospital, but rather ahead of me in the everyday business of living, my joy in all that good health was somewhat diminished.

I was self-conscious, tentative and afraid that any move I made was bound to be a bad one. This restricted the emotional room I permitted myself for people to enter into my life or for me to enter theirs. I merely glanced off the surface of this person or that with a growing sense of discontent. My new life wasn't much different from the old.

During my fat years, I had hidden my vulnerability behind an excess of ambition to be the best conductor on Broadway, the cleverest person in the crowd, and had developed a domineering manner barely short of provoking overt antagonism. I had shed the fat, but not the vulnerability. I was still lonely.

The answer, of course, was to expose myself honestly and take my chances. But I couldn't simply will myself to feel and behave differently. And certainly not alone.

I needed somebody, a special somebody whom I could care about, somebody with whom I could exchange intimate feelings.

The solution, I mumbled to myself, is simple. Look in the yellow pages under Somebody or Special.

The phone rang. Could A.T.&T. be so efficient that having tapped my mind and overheard my mumble, they were already sending help?

"Hello."

"Herbert?"

The voice was familiar, but the "Herbert" was unique. People undoubtedly had many names for me. The most enduring four-letter one was Herb. But one, and only one, person called me Herbert: Carolyn Jones.

"Carolyn?!" I said excitedly.

"Yes. How are you? How do you feel?"

"What are you doing in New York? Or are you calling from the Coast?"

"No, I'm here."

"God, it's good to hear your voice. How are you?

How long will you be staying?" I ran on in the momentum of delight.

"In order of questions asked," she said, laughing, "I'm fine and I'll be here for a week. Now, tell me about you."

"Oh, I'm in great shape. And I want to thank you again for all the flowers and books you sent while I was boning up on walking."

"Oooh, Herbert," she said, wincing audibly. "But your thank-you notes were funny. I used to bring them to the studio and read them to everybody. One producer told me that if you had written a few 'Addams Family' shows, I'd still be playing Morticia, God forbid!"

"Tell me, are you here for business or pleasure?"

"Both, I hope. I've been offered the national tour of *The Homecoming*. Have you seen it?"

"No. But I hear it's one hell of a play."

"Can you come with me tonight? I know it's short notice, but I want to see you, if you're free. It's been such a long time."

"You've gone and done it again, Carolyn."

"Done what?"

"Shined up the streets, that's all."

"What are you raving about?"

"Here I was looking forward to a clammy July evening with nothing to do except admire the air-conditioner, and wham! You show up, and even the sidewalks of New York look good to me. How about dinner at Sardi's before the show?"

"Great idea, but my publicity people sicced their

local dragon lady on me for some movie magazine shots this afternoon. I'll be hugging street lights until about six."

"Then I'll pick you up at six thirty. Oh, I better warn you that I'm not quite the same as when you saw me last."

"What is it? Are your legs all right?"

"My legs are fine. It's the rest of me that's different. I lost a hundred pounds."

"A hundred pounds? I'm dying to see what you look like."

"Where are you staying?"

"I'm at the Essex House."

"I'll be there at six thirty. And thanks for calling. Goodbye, Carolyn."

"Bye, Herbert."

Her call was so beautifully timed that I wondered if A.T.&T. weren't responsible after all. I stuck my nose out the window to test the weather and was pleasantly surprised at the springlike day spawned by a departing July. Perhaps as a gesture of apology for all the sweat it had left in its wake.

"George," I said out loud doing a little jig, "George, you wholesale dealer in aching bodies and joints, you should see me now. I'm going to walk an extra mile today. I'm at my best."

Then I recalled George's reply to an earlier boast:

"That's the best so far. But not the best you'll ever do except if you drop dead now."

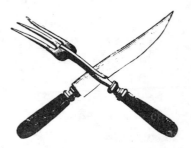

On my way to pick up Carolyn, I thought how unusual it was that we went from a professional relationship to a close friendship and never even noticed when or how.

We saw each other through some difficult times and shared the fun when things went well, but never did that friendship change to anything more intimate by so much as a gesture. In Carolyn, I now had my somebody special to whom I could spill anything without fear or embarrassment.

My spirits reached great heights and then, inexplicably, they plummeted. I felt glum, abandoned and lonely again. After all, she'd only be in town for a few days and then where would I be? By the time I got to the Essex House, I was almost sorry she'd come East to begin with.

On the way up to her room I kicked myself for such

a rabid thought and made a note to take a saliva test at the local dog pound.

When Carolyn answered the door, I drew myself up like a Victorian suitor and recited:

> Roses are red,
> Violets are blue,
> I like cymbidiums
> So I brought some for you.
> But to be on the safe side,
> I brought a rose too.

She laughed delightedly and gave me a bear hug. "Cymbidiums! Oh, you remembered! God, how I love cymbidiums. They're beautiful. And so is the rose. And"—she held me at arm's length—"Herbert Greene, so are you. I can't decide whether to kiss the cymbidiums and admire you or vice versa. You're gorgeous. Come on in."

She was wearing a colorful floor-length dress that revealed her classic frame. The look was as smooth as rich wine in clear crystal. We began our usual mile-a-minute talk, talk, talk as though we hadn't been apart for more than a year. And barely got going, it seemed, when it was time to leave.

Sardi's impeccable maitre d', Jimmy, seated us and quickly saw to it that our order was taken. Carolyn and I picked at our food. The tempo of our talk increased, as we reverted to a shorthand speech we had developed over years of familiarity. Sudden shifts of subjects were easily accommodated and often anticipated. During an exchange about the relative merits of deafness as a fitting reward for rock 'n' roll, I said:

"It's the damndest thing, but since I've lost all that weight, I seem to be more sensitive to people staring at me than I was when I was a balloon."

She cocked her head and pinned me with those big blue eyes.

"You mean you're mad at your friends?"

I considered that for a moment.

"I never thought about it. But, yes, you're right. That's it. I am."

"And I'll bet you walk by a mirror and wonder who that stranger is."

"Oh, that one. Even when I stop and look, I'm not sure."

"Bet you get boiling mad when women suddenly pay you a great deal of attention. Especially the women who hardly noticed you when you were heavy."

"Boiling and steaming. Say, you know a hell of a lot about this for someone who never went through it."

"But I did."

"I can't picture you ever being fat."

"I wasn't. My cross was a big nose. Very long and very unattractive. Let's say I wasn't overwhelmed with boy friends. But after my nose job, the guys were all over me, opening doors, sending flowers, and my telephone was ringing off the wall."

"That must have made you feel good."

"It made me feel terrible. I wanted people to like me for me, and not because my nose was fixed. Why should my smaller nose make such a big difference? I got so wild that I wanted to scream at everybody sending flowers: Where were you when I needed one rose?"

"You were right, absolutely right."

"I was wrong, absolutely wrong."

"I don't get it. You aren't simply a nose. You're a human being."

"Listen, Herbert. There are billions of human beings. But when I got my nose fixed, I became a much better looking human being. Attractive, if you will. And, being attractive, I attracted. But I didn't know how to deal with that. I had a new nose, but I was the old me. I resented everybody who noticed the change for the better. Because it made me feel that they hadn't seen anything worthwhile in me before. I'd have given anything if I could have grown my nose back. But when strangers began to pay attention too, I had nothing to feel angry about. After all, they didn't reject me when my nose was long. So I got a big clue. I needed to cut out all the junk that stood in the way of accepting myself—all the junk that had been there with the old nose."

"I guess I need some inside physiotherapy too. Isn't that what you mean?"

"I mean it makes no sense to say: Listen folks, I've changed, but pay no attention or you're all admitting you never liked me before anyway."

Her words buzzed like so many bees around the honeycomb made by my nerves.

"You've given me a lot to think about, Carolyn, and I'm very grateful."

She threw up her hands, simulating fright.

"Oh, no! Oh, no! Do you know how many friendships have been spoiled by gratitude?"

"I don't know. But I won't let this one be."

Jimmy, the ever helpful maitre d', wandered over.

"If you and Miss Jones are on your way to the theater, Mr. Greene, it's getting close to curtain time."

Thanking him, I called for the check. On our way out, I was astonished to discover how uncomfortable I felt at the waving celebrities, the observant media people and the gawking civilians who recognized Carolyn at once.

Only when I found myself virtually pressing up to Carolyn, a most uncharacteristic lapse of taste on my part, did I discover that I was desperately trying to conceal something.

My fat belly! The fat belly that was no longer fat, no longer ballooning out in front of me to tempt the side-view mirrors of passing taxicabs. I reacted to this discovery like a paranoid schizophrenic.

On the one hand, I chided myself for such absurd and furtive behavior; there was, simply and factually, no fat belly to hide. On the other hand, I was certain I had been hallucinating all along that I was not a fat man, and defended my ridiculous attempt to hide as not only reasonable, but mandatory, if I were to avoid unbearable humiliation. Worse still, I found nothing unnatural in the sheer insanity of this paradox.

Then I was struck by the fact that what Carolyn had told me only a little earlier seemed to have gone in one ear and out the other. Maybe my inside physio-therapy would take a bit longer than a few minutes.

Harold Pinter's *The Homecoming* seemed to make no more sense to the audience than my earlier behavior did to me. The central character, a woman, pitted against five emotionally imprisoned men, deliberately acts out what each man has predetermined she is or has been. Her real identity is irrelevant and remains concealed.

I felt a peculiar rapport with this strange play, perversely identifying with it. In my own emotional lock-up I was still fat, regardless of the fact that my body was not. What was the reality? The deeply imbedded conviction of what I once had been, or my objective appearance as it had now become? My disturbance grew even as the final curtain fell. I wondered whether Carolyn might ever have had a similar experience. But I felt I had spent enough time on myself already.

"Let's go back to my hotel to talk," she said as we left the theater. "I'd like to hear what you think about the play. And besides, my damn eyelashes are coming unstuck."

"O.K. If we run like hell for Eighth Avenue, we can beat the mob for a cab."

The minute we entered her suite, she peeled off her eyelashes, breathed a sigh of relief and said, "These are no longer my favorite eyelashes, they hurt."

When we were comfortable and sipping drinks, Carolyn asked reflectively, "Do you think I should do this play?"

"You can play it like a dream, if that's what you mean."

"Yes, I think I could, too. But it is a challenge. And it would be my first time in a Broadway play. But won't the audiences be expecting Morticia and getting Pinter instead?"

"But you've played a hell of a lot of parts since 'The Addams Family.' Have there been any complaints? The real question is how you feel about the show and the tour."

She hesitated.

"The truth is that I'm not sure how I feel because of a personal thing. I've been involved with somebody and we've talked about getting married as soon as we were sure. Well, I'm not sure. And these last few weeks I've been feeling less and less sure. But I haven't been able to discuss it with him. I'm afraid I'll hurt him. The pressure's gotten so bad that I jumped at the chance to come East when I was offered the job. But what's making me miserable is I might accept the tour just to run away. I don't trust myself."

I remembered George, who never tired of telling me that sympathy might feel good, but doing something felt better. I told her what I thought.

"O.K. So you're guilty about running away. So you're ashamed of being a coward. That doesn't give you a corner on the very-evil-person market. Sometimes running away is the only good thing you can do. At least you get some distance. If you really want to marry the guy, you have a much better chance to find out when you're not under the gun."

"You mean like in 'absence makes the heart grow fonder'?"

I shrugged.

"Or like in 'out of sight, out of mind.' Take your choice. But at least give yourself the chance to make the choice."

She turned the idea over. Then, as though thinking out loud, she said, "That sounds right. That really sounds right. But it sure is selfish."

"Sure it's selfish. But would you rather be unselfishly miserable for the rest of your life?"

She sighed.

"But is it fair? If I do the play, I'll hurt him badly. And then if I decide I want to marry him later on, I'll feel guilty for having behaved so selfishly."

"I think you ought to keep the fair-unfair thing out of it. Because if fair-unfair is on your mind, you're going to feel that either he hurts you or you hurt him, or you both hurt each other."

"There must be another way without hurting or being hurt."

"There is. Do both. Marry the man and do the show too."

"That's ridiculous. I already told you I'm not sure I want to marry him. Show or no show."

"Then, Carolyn, you're back to square one, which really amounts to one choice: Take the show now and worry about your marriage later."

She shook her head, frowning angrily.

"That's no choice at all. That's running away. And I hate that. No, I won't do it."

"That sounds more like stubbornness than worrying about what's fair," I said impatiently.

"And you sound like a top sergeant chewing out a subordinate."

"I'm sorry, Carolyn. I didn't mean it that way."

"Oh, damn! It's me who should be sorry," she said regretfully. "You haven't done anything except to be honest."

"Well, sleep on it. We can talk tomorrow." I finished my drink and soon left.

The next morning I took a break from some orchestrations I was doing and went to Saks Fifth Avenue. I bought a half-dozen pairs of assorted eyelashes and included a note:

Twelve lashes for insubordination.
H.G.

That afternoon, Carolyn signed her contract to tour in Pinter's play and cut short her New York visit. With only two weeks before the start of rehearsals, she had to close her house and attend to a blizzard of odds and ends. When I saw her off, I was so far behind in my own work that I considered quitting the job and sending a dignified note of apology, followed by a quiet suicide and modest interment.

By a tremendous show of guilt and cowardice I scared myself into the discovery that five hours of sleep was all I needed to complete a seventy-two-hour trial of endurance. I finished orchestrating right under the wire and topped it off with a twelve-hour recording session. Afterward, I slept for two days. The following day, Carolyn called.

"I'm back," she exulted.

"How did you manage to settle everything in one week?"

"That was easy. I decided that I wanted a week to have some fun and see something of New York," she said. "So I told my housekeeper what had to be done, sent out my itinerary to everybody who might need it and just took off. And, oh yes, my personal problem worked out beautifully. I simply said my piece and it turned out that neither one of us wanted to get married. I owe you a great deal for that."

It felt good talking to her again. I didn't wait for her to invite me to see her.

"Are you busy for lunch tomorrow?" I asked.

"No," she answered.

"Great. We ought to decide what time to have our dinner tonight so that we can arrange the exact time for lunch tomorrow."

"What was that?"

"Well, it's very New Yorky to have dinner as an appetizer for lunch the next day."

Sometime during the lunches and dinners that followed, our friendship flared into love: a man-woman butterflies-in-the-belly kind of love that hit us both very hard. By Wednesday, I was dreaming we were engaged. By Thursday, I was thinking we were married. And by Friday, I had gained ten pounds.

It happened so insidiously that I never knew how and when it was going on. Little things did it. Like having regular lunches instead of my usual black coffee and cottage cheese. Enjoying a cocktail or two with Carolyn before dinner, and dinner itself. Not wild and especially crazy dinners. Just dinners. Steak-salad-baked-potato-no-dessert-type dinners. Carolyn rarely ate more than half of what was served, often less. I finished every morsel.

I also found myself nibbling at crackers and rolls while sipping cocktails before ordering dinner. And if the food took some time in arriving, the nibbling would increase. And, when feeling especially good or expansive, I'd spring for a dessert. As our mealtimes became more intimate, they stretched out considerably. This naturally led to a lovely variety of after-dinner liqueurs and brandies.

I discovered that falling in love enhanced all my appetites. Carolyn was rather more selective. Food was less attractive to her than the romantic settings of New York's finest and most charming restaurants.

I told myself that when the next week rolled around and she began her daily grueling rehearsals, I'd be so miserable at being separated from her I would easily mourn away those ten lousy pounds.

The weeks that now ensued were a classic example of Einstein's theory of relativity. Spending so many hours without Carolyn caused me to view time differently. After a week's gallop, it wanted some rest. It was always yawning, stretching out and taking frequent naps.

But no matter how hard I worked to fill in the hours around the time I spent with Carolyn, there was always a glut of hours left over.

I gained twenty pounds in those weeks, making a grand total of thirty pounds. Thirty pounds of flesh and blood that was me, yet felt as though a stranger had taken possession of my face, my neck, my arms, my legs and my will. I was so shocked by this unanticipated invasion that I wasn't able to act. Instead of dividing and conquering my excess weight pound by pound, I found myself merely wishing for a way to get rid of it in one reverse swallow.

This trouble created another. I no longer wanted to be seen in public.

But show business was no business to be in if I wanted anonymity. With Carolyn starring in her first Broadway show, the social and professional demands on her were constant: endless rounds of newspaper and TV interviews, and many glamorous parties where the cream of show business would be thickened by the smooth blenders of the political world.

I simply had to find a way of avoiding the torture of public exposure. Six days before Carolyn was to leave New York and begin her tour, I hit upon the obvious solution of the noble deception. In plain English, subterfuge. In plainer English, a damn lie.

"Carolyn, darling, I've been thinking. This tour isn't going to be a vacation. Before you've even unpacked in one town, you're scrambling on to the next. I think you ought to start pacing yourself now."

"Don't worry about me, darling, I'm having the time of my life."

Her eyes shone. Still, I found it more important to dim that light than to continue to expose my growing bulk.

"Sure, this is a great time for you. But I just can't help worrying that with a raw Eastern winter on the way, and you running yourself ragged, your asthma might kick up again."

She flinched.

"God, just the thought of that gives me the creeps."

She reached out and touched my face.

"Thank you for thinking about me."

If I squirmed under her loving gaze, her next move made me feel like a card-carrying Nazi. She picked up the phone and cancelled a half-dozen glittering engagements.

"There," she said, "how's that for openers?"

The skinny man who is locked up in every fat man didn't scream to be let out. Instead, he groaned helplessly, and judging by the nasty spasm in my gut, collapsed.

The following day being Wednesday, Carolyn had a matinee. After dropping her at the theater, I stopped to pick up a couple of corned beef sandwiches. I'd need some sustenance if I was to finish an orchestration that I had let ride dangerously close to the deadline. Like my nobility, this habit was also a newly emerging facet of my character.

By the time I got home I was ravenous. Since the dining-room table also served as a writing desk, I hastily brushed the music paper aside to make room for my plate. Wanting the greatest freedom, I tore off my clothes and sat down to eat.

After a couple of bites, I got that nasty feeling of being watched. I looked up. It was true. The oversized mirror on the wall revealed me to myself: naked, hunched over my plate, clutching the remains of a sandwich in one hand, while the other encircled my plate protectively, a fair picture of Neanderthal man fiercely guarding his kill.

In the next instant, I became furious. I defiantly resumed eating and engaged in a stare-down battle with the goddamn glass. I swiftly bit and devoured the corned beef, as though a show of teeth would intimidate the mirror. But when the sandwiches were gone, I was without the distraction of chewing and swallowing, and left with stark confrontation. I tried to glance at the half-finished music, but I was mesmerized by the mirror, mirror on the wall and helplessly pinned in place.

At that moment, the skinny man inside me struck.

"Hey, Fatso," he summoned me crudely.

I didn't move a muscle.

"Yeah, I mean you."

"Go away," I forced myself to answer.

"No. I want to ask you a few questions."

"Later."

"Now."

"What questions?"

"If you're so serious about Carolyn Jones, why do you pick such a funny way to show it?"

"Get lost."

"Fatso," said my skinny nemesis, "you can get devious or you can get to the point, but you can't tell me to get lost in this lock-up."

He wouldn't give an inch, so I tried to mollify him.

"All right, all right. I lied to her. Everybody in love lies. I'll apologize."

"Oh, no you don't," he pounced like a cat. "Lying

was only part of what you did. What about the rest of it?"

I clammed up, threatened that any minute the corned beef would come up hash.

"O.K., Fatso. Just answer yes or no. Aren't those show business parties used more to promote future deals than for socializing?" 1797465

"Yes."

"And didn't you jeopardize Carolyn's career by gaslighting her into cancelling these opportunities?"

"Yes."

"And didn't you behave in this appalling way only because you're a glutton trying to make like an ostrich?"

That finally broke me.

"Yes, yes, yes. I'm a fat slob. I'm too embarrassed to be seen in public and I'm afraid to admit it to her. I'm chicken, I've got closets full of white feathers, all right?"

"All wrong, Fatso. You're only confessing so you won't have to look at the reason you have something to confess."

"Ah, what's the use," I whined, "even when I admit the truth, you don't believe me."

"The truth?" My skinny prosecutor laughed, causing me a painful hiccough. "You're about as close to the truth as a pig is to kosher."

Enough was enough, I decided.

"If I'm so far from the truth, you must be pretty near it yourself. So let's have it. Put up or shut up."

"O.K., Fatso, but a little bit at a time. Even *your*

appetite couldn't stomach it all at once. Ready?"

"Yeah, I'm ready."

"You're strongly attracted to this girl, right?"

"Right."

"Did you ever hear of a three-hundred-pound great lover? And if you did, wouldn't you break your head trying to figure out the angles?"

"I don't have such sexual fantasies."

"Try 'em. If you keep going this way, you're gonna need 'em."

"And that's your big-type truth?"

"Wait. That's not all. If you were a junkie or a drunk, that would hurt Carolyn more, wouldn't it?"

"What the hell are you driving at now?"

"You're no better than a drug addict or an alcoholic."

"What?" I retorted indignantly. "But those people are crazy. They'll do anything for a fix or a slug of juice. Steal. Pimp. Whore. Anything."

"And what would you do if your eating habit cost you a hundred dollars a day? You'd steal. Pimp. Whore. Anything. That's right. Anything. Get off your high horse, Fatso, before you give the poor animal a hernia."

I had nothing but black coffee for three days. When Carolyn didn't remark on this oddity, my feelings were hurt. I decided to bring it to her attention.

"Darling?" I began tentatively.

"Yes?"

"Darling, uh, have you noticed anything strange these last couple of days?"

"Strange-peculiar or strange-exotic?"

"You could say both."

"Well, it's strange-peculiar it took us so long to know what a strange-exotic pair we make."

That, I knew, could lead to anything but what I had in mind at the moment.

"Haven't you found it strange that I've been drinking so much black coffee?" I asked. This sounded stupid even as it came out, but she considered it.

"No. But if it bothers you, don't drink so much."

I grew desperate and simply blurted out: "I quit eating!"

Her eyes widened a fraction, then she burst into laughter.

"You mean like cigarettes?"

"I'm not kidding," I said, agitated.

"Herbert, honey, what's wrong?"

"There's thirty pounds of what's wrong. That's just to begin with."

"Oh, that," she said in relief, "I know that. I noticed it last week. But I think it's kind of . . . well . . . cuddly. I like it."

It was exasperating that she didn't take the same view of the problem I did. I had to awaken her to the insane compulsion that drove me, that consumed so much of my thoughts, energy and time. So I bluntly told her how I had lied to her, and why.

She took her time as my words sank in.

"But what were you afraid of?"

"I was afraid I'd look ridiculous in your eyes if we were seen out together."

"But that doesn't make sense. What possible difference could it make whether we see each other alone or in public?"

Her question startled me.

"I don't know. I just felt it wasn't safe for me if we went out. I can't even explain it now."

She looked closely at me.

"Were you worried that people would think we were a mismatch? And sooner or later I'd begin to feel that way too?"

I nodded miserably.

"I suppose so."

"I'm so sorry," she said sadly. "But I guess I was too busy worrying about myself. I've been afraid that you were only attracted to me because of my quote, movie star image, unquote. It's happened before."

"You worried about that?" I asked incredulously. "But why?? We've been friends for so many years that I just assumed you trusted me to see beyond the image. I admired you as an actress. But it was a real blood-and-flesh woman that I reached out for. There's no movie star image between me and the real you. Trust me."

She was silent for awhile, but did not seem to be quiet from within.

"But can't you trust me to see into and love the real you?"

"The trouble is that I'm not quite sure who the real me is. After all, I didn't become a brand-new man because of something I did all on my own. It was an accident. And in the hospital, I had no choice. But now,

I've got to make the change stick, all alone. And the first time I stumble, I lie to cover up."

"Darling, you're not all alone. You have me. And as for the lie"—she smiled—"as you once told me, sometimes people have to run away from the truth to be able to make a choice. And you've done that. You're back to your diet and you told me the truth. That should prove the new you is real."

"But what if I stumble again? I don't want to come to you as a defeated man, but as somebody who respects himself. Then I can feel I've earned your respect."

"Darling, I hope for the rest of our lives we fight to keep each other's respect. And if we stumble once in a while, it won't matter."

I felt a tremendous surge of elation. I wasn't alone. And I didn't have to be ashamed if I needed her help. As long as I knew she wanted me, there was nothing I couldn't do. And because I wanted and needed her even more, the possibility of turning back was out of the question.

After Carolyn's departure for Philadelphia, I doggedly stuck with my black coffee and dropped six pounds. That left twenty-four more to burn off, twenty-four pounds that looked to me as though they had been patched onto my frame by a drunken sculptor of the abstract expressionist school.

To meet another deadline, I began an eighteen-hour-a-day schedule, writing a blizzard of notes. I became a fanatic for black coffee and work.

By the end of the week I knocked off another six pounds. I took off, headed due southwest for Philly as Carolyn and I planned, made it to the Forrest Theater by 9:30 P.M. and was waiting in her dressing room for the Act One curtain of *The Homecoming* to ring down.

Our reunion was so enthusiastic that she barely made her second-act curtain. After the show, we had what was left of Saturday plus the whole Sunday.

We used our thirty-six hours like a pair of spendthrift misers, hoarding our time and extravagant with our strength by the simple expedient of not sleeping. We talked endlessly about what to do after her tour. Her career was in Movieland, mine in New York, a difference of three thousand miles.

Without arriving at conclusions, we agreed that we'd crack that nut when the time came. So, another farewell and another pair of upper lips that didn't quite manage to remain stiff, and off I clattered on the rails back to New York.

I was dog tired when I fell into bed, but I couldn't fall asleep. I had a sense of something important being wrong. Very wrong. After stewing for awhile, I reviewed the weekend.

Then it hit me. While in Philadelphia, I had not only eaten hefty room-service meals, but had drinks to boot. My diet was shot to hell. I shuddered at the thought of the miserable number I knew would turn up on the face of the scale on the bathroom floor. Defeated, I fell asleep.

"Hey, Fatso."

"Shut up," I hollered, shooting fully awake as my diaphragm tightened to support my yell. My skinny prisoner was at it again.

"C'mon, wake up, Fatso."

"I'm up, dammit!"

"I want to talk."

"At this hour?" I groaned.

"It's ten o'clock in the morning. Quit stalling."

I sat up and leaned against the headboard, resigned.

"Do you know your Webster, Fatso?"

"My what?"

"Webster. You know, like in dictionary."

"I'm familiar with it," I said sourly.

"Good. Define obese."

"Obese is fat."

"That is a colloquial synonym. I said define it, Fatso."

"Obese," I recited like a schoolboy, "having a graceless and often unhealthy excess of flesh."

"Very good, Fatso. Now can you make some reasonable assumptions that would have led Webster to such a definition?"

"Sure. Webster was a sadist."

"Irrelevant, Fatso. I asked for some reasonable assumptions."

"Sorry, I gave my last one away yesterday."

"Look, Fatso, is it a reasonable assumption that a graceless and unhealthy excess of food leads to obesity?"

"Yes."

"Is it a reasonable assumption that nobody wants to appear graceless?"

"Yes."

"Is it a reasonable assumption that nobody wants to be unhealthy?"

"Yes."

"Now, Fatso, that's enough information upon which to draw some reasonable conclusions. Care to draw some?"

"Yes. I'd like to conclude you."

"You can't. I am you."

I had waltzed right into that shaft.

"Tell you what, Fatso. Since you're fresh out of

reasonable conclusions, you're welcome to mine. Would you try a rational approach to an irrational person threatening you with a knife or would you just take it away from him by any means?"

"I don't get the connection."

"Being obese is irrational. And food in your hands is the weapon. Disarm yourself, Fatso, disarm."

"Well, goddammit, I try to diet."

"That's a rational approach, Fatso. But remember, you are a compulsive, irrational and armed menace. Fight fire with fire."

"You mean I should become even more irrational? You're crazy."

"No. You are. But not crazy enough. Not by a half. Your only chance is to manage the other half. See you around."

As unexpectedly as he arrived, my skinny prisoner vanished. And although I preferred to live without his visits, this time I wanted him to tell me more. What the hell did he mean? After tussling with myself for an hour, I got a bad headache and decided he was out of his mind. Now if I could only get him out of mine.

Four months went by: a period in which I rode a seesaw built for one. My weight went up and down, up and down, but without rhythm or balance. Because each week the previous low was not quite reached, while the previous high was always broken.

This must not be permitted to go on, I sternly told myself. I had to get a grip on myself.

So I began to circle the bathroom scale. Instead of weighing myself regularly, I only did so when I was certain I had lost a few pounds. But that was hardly soothing since those lost pounds began obeying the law of diminishing returns.

Insidiously, the idea grew that the bathroom was making a nervous wreck of me and should therefore be avoided whenever possible. This led to some exotic experiments. I initiated a unique game of beard growing. In between professional engagements, I would surprise myself with seeing how a week's growth would look at first glance.

In order to do this, I kept the door of the medicine cabinet ajar and pasted newspaper over the large mirror in my dining-room study. This unique mirror treatment brought me the additional bonus of not having to look at any part of my swelling body.

I shunned all social intercourse with the exception of unavoidable professional contacts. I quit the restaurant circuit too, ordered all my food by telephone and packed my freezer to the gills in order to evade the probing eyes of too many delivery boys.

I also began to skip daily bathing or showering, under the righteous banner of rebellion against the barrage of commercials that implied Americans were an evil-smelling race. And I gloated when three bathless days would go by without giving offense to myself.

In short, I became Herbert the High Hermit. As Carolyn's tour took her even farther west, our weekends became less frequent. On the occasions we did manage, she didn't seem to notice the steady rise in my weight. Nor did she raise an eyebrow at the liquor and meals I consumed.

I not only drank and ate, but cursed myself more than usual for each bite and swallow. I found I could tolerate myself better after three or four drinks, re-assuring myself that I'd start to drop all the excess baggage the minute I came home.

As my failure to reduce became more noticeable, and my pants threatened me with a double hernia, I took to cancelling those rare weekends when we could have gotten together by inventing crushingly tight deadlines for nonexistent jobs. The excuse I offered to myself was that I deserved retribution because I was committing the heinous sin of gluttony. Naturally, I did not deal with the deprivation I caused Carolyn, the innocent victim of my version of crime and punishment.

I paid the price of the long-distance lover, hitting a peak of $2,300 for one month of phone calls.

Saddled with the shameful burden of stalling my sweet, loving Carolyn, I got deeper and deeper into thinner and thinner lies. But she never uttered a word of reproach. Yet I could sense the growing bewilderment, the hurt between her words, as I broke date after date after date.

By the end of this four-month period, I had put back fifty-six of the original hundred pounds I had dropped.

Sealing myself off produced a predictable side effect. The demand for Herbert Greene's social presence diminished noticeably.

After a week of utter silence, my telephone rang. It was an old pal from Hollywood, Rock Hudson.

"Hi, Herb," his rich voice came over the wire. "How ya been?"

"Rock! What are you doing in Fun City?"

"Oh, somebody wants me to do a musical. Do you know David Merrick?"

"Sure, very well."

"I'd like to talk to you about this show."

"Any time."

"I'm throwing a party tomorrow night, can you come? I know it's short notice but I just decided."

Party. I shuddered. Then I remembered that Rock hadn't seen me since before my accident, before I lost those hundred pounds, so the regained fifty-six would make it look to him as though I was losing weight.

"With pleasure. My calendar is clear." So clear I could see forever, I thought bitterly.

He gave me the address and rang off with, "The boozing starts at eight thirty."

After I hung up, I panicked. My clothes would fit me well enough if I could learn to enjoy strangulation. I had little time and less inclination to buy anything new. I could have killed myself for throwing away my fat clothes during a seizure of smugness.

While worrying that bone, I remembered saving one complete "fat" outfit as a reminder of what I once was. I scrambled through the closet and found it: a dark pin-striped suit, shirt and tie to match. I tried it on. Too big. But better to turn an embarrassed red than a suffocated blue, I philosophized.

On my way to the party, I fought repeated impulses to turn tail and slink back to my hermitage. I tried practicing a few ad libs. But all I could think of was:

> Herbert Greene is so obese,
> That where he's sat you'll find a crease.

I had to fight off the maddening rhyme, which went around and around in my head. I was frantic that the damn thing would practice itself to perfection and pop out at the first lull in conversation.

I rang the bell at 8:45 and was admitted by a liveried Arthur Treacher type whose "Good evening, sir, this way please," was the perfect blend of nose-wrinkling disdain and mild deference.

Crossing the vestibule, whose enormous proportions

would have done for a living room in most ordinary apartments, I was impressed with its spare appointments, proving that it wasn't necessary to cram a room with a great volume of things to authenticate the owner's means, just as it wasn't necessary to consume tubs of caviar to prove one could afford it.

Before I could shake the irritability brought on by this comparison, I was ushered into an immense living room. The guests were standing around in loose clusters. A whole length of glass wall revealed the nocturnal city, its million lights sparkling like so many sugar-frosted jewels.

The effect was especially calming to me: It made me feel small. I could almost feel my bulk and girth shrink.

A clap on the back jolted me and I turned to see Rock smiling a welcome.

"Hi, Herb. You look great. By God, you must have lost a ton of weight."

I twitched and smiled and uttered inanities as I checked to make sure my coat was buttoned. Baggy big as it was, it hid my frontal outbreak of fat.

I grabbed a drink from the tray of a passing waiter and tossed it off in two swallows while I directed Rock's attention to the panorama.

"If you're not too busy," he said, "would you read the script and listen to the music of this show Merrick has in mind?"

"Sure," I said, beckoning the waiter and exchanging my empty for another blast.

"Great. I'll have the script sent to you."

At this point, a gang of Hollywood glamour converged on us. Robert Wagner, Angela Lansbury, Louis Jourdan, Jean Simmons, people I hadn't seen for more than a year. Friendly and flattering in their greetings, not one of them missed a gracious compliment about my weight loss.

Bob Wagner threw an arm around my shoulder and said to the group:

"I've tried three times to teach Herb golf. He's the only man in the history of the game who knocked himself half cold with his own ball."

I stopped listening as a waiter went by with a beautiful tray of savory hors d'oeuvres that almost tore my eyes from their sockets. In these circumstances, there was no way, absolutely no way to attack them. I could only follow their tantalizing line of flight.

". . . so the ball squirts out with lots of English, caroms off his golf club and wham! Herb gets beaned with his own golf ball."

Everybody doubled up in laughter. I was getting stoned and beginning to believe that I was what all these nice people had said: really slimming down. But my eyes kept raping the passing trays of hors d'oeuvres.

We were now joined by two newcomers, Lee Remick and Robert Preston. Both looked at me for a moment and burst out in unison:

"My God! What's happened to you?"

Preston, who had seen me just a few months back minus fifty-six pounds, was understandably flabbergasted. Lee Remick, however, was judging by a much weightier standard.

How I shifted the stricken look that passed between

Preston and myself to one of modest acceptance of Lee's compliment will remain a mystery forever, but it was a fine example of strength through desperation. Preston recovered in nothing flat. The discipline of the actor was evident as he appeared to echo Lee's delighted surprise.

Hours later, after consuming an enormous dinner, I was still feeling rotten. Since I had also consumed a like amount of liquor, I should have been feeling no pain. No pain at all.

In the middle of somebody's remarks, perhaps even my own, I followed a sudden impulse to leave. Tearing loose from my chair with surprising ease, because I was only leaning against it, I simply walked out without a goodnight to anyone.

The taxi ride home was extraordinary. With every lurch or bump I almost exploded. Because both my upper and lower digestive tracts were packed tight, sudden motion threatened me with a unique physiological phenomenon: the simultaneous onset of forward and reverse peristalsis.

Whichever muscular brakes I applied to control one imminent eruption automatically set its opposite in motion. This physical paradox couldn't be rationalized away. The two halves of the paradox chipped away at each other and inevitably struck a spark. Lodging in my highly volatile, paranoid mind, it ignited a firestorm. I bitterly condemned my host for serving contaminated food, diagnosing my misery as ptomaine poisoning or botulism or both.

In any case, I'd have bet my life the autopsy would show it was something I ate.

I entered my apartment furious at my craven acceptance of Rock's invitation. He could take his show and that abominable showman, David Merrick, and stuff 'em.

I emphasized each outburst by slamming down pieces of clothing I was ripping off. These also received my aggrieved attention.

Goddamn heavy jacket.

Dumb tie.

Miserable shirt.

Halfway out of my pants, the phone rang.

"Now, what?!!" I bellowed at it.

I rolled onto the floor, and after kicking myself into a hopeless tangle, was forced to snake my way to the ringing phone.

"Hello," I barked when I finally reached it.

"Oh, darling, you're home. I was about to hang up."

"Of course I'm home," I answered irritably, wondering who the hell I was talking to.

"How are you, darling?"

The telltale miniature chimes against a background of white noise signaled a long-distance call.

"Honey? Herbert? Are you still there?"

"Carolyn?" I ventured stupidly.

"Oh, darling, forgive me. You sound as though you were fast asleep."

"No, oh, no. Boy, I miss you."

"Me too. I wish I could dive into the phone and zip over."

For a split second, I believed she could. I instinctively tried to hide my rounded belly by pulling my knees up in fetal position. Then I relaxed.

"It'll be years before they invent that. But I wish you could."

"Do you, really?"

Her voice sounded so near and warm I almost cried. "Especially tonight, Carolyn. God, how I needed you tonight, Carolyn."

"What happened? Are you all right?"

A warning gong clanged in my head, but I managed to ignore it.

"Oh, I'm all right, I guess. Did you know that dinner parties are a dumber invention than television?"

After a slight pause, she replied tentatively, "You mean, it was lonely for you?"

"Christ! Lonely? It was impossible! Imagine trying to eat dinner with a table full of people counting every bite you take."

Another pause.

"Herbert, are you a little crocked?"

"No. I am definitely not a little crocked. I am a whole lot crocked."

She laughed.

"Oh, that explains a lot. Do you want to tell me what really happened?"

"What I told you was what really happened. That's why I got bombed."

"You're not making much sense, baby."

"Well, there was this dinner party. I was hungry as hell. And they hardly gave me enough to get a pygmy off the ground. So I had to fend for myself. And those smart asses at my table just picked and fooled around with their stuff, and gave me a lot of evil eye because I finished first and went back for measly seconds. Anyway, I hate eating in public. I can't relax. I hate to make believe that food is to talk-all-the-latest-old-news-over instead of to eat. Jesus! They make you feel like a degenerate or something if you eat dinner at a dinner party. Know what I mean?"

"I know exactly," she said soothingly. "I hate it when they serve so late that I get stoned just waiting. Poor thing, you probably had to wait until midnight to get fed."

The warning gong re-sounded the alarm. It only irritated me.

"No, you don't understand. Dinner was early enough, and enough to feed an army. It was those people watching me. I can't stand a bunch of people sitting around watching me eat. That's all."

"Why don't you go to sleep, honey. I'm sure you'll feel better in the morning."

"Maybe. How's the trip? Touring isn't too great, is it?"

"It's fine. Just fine."

"Bet you're beat and homesick. How's the room service? Food okay? Send it back if it's not good."

"Don't worry about me, honey. I'm all right. You go to bed. And call me tomorrow. Remember, I'm in San Francisco. So there's a three-hour time difference."

"Sure, I know. I'll call you tomorrow. I'm kind of hungry, come to think of it. I'll just get a bite and flake out. Bye."

After hanging up, I huffed and puffed through the tangle I'd made of my clothing. Once free, however, I remained on the floor simply because there was no place else I wanted to go.

I got a belated reaction to Carolyn's phone call. As I rehashed it, the previously ignored warning gong sounded like the clang of the forge. Now I heeded it. Repeatedly. I had second, third and fourth thoughts about that call. Yet each time the threat of clarity raised its head, I submerged it in contemplation of the swirling designs in the weave of the rug.

Another thought nudged me. The fridge. I had to check the fridge. Wrenching free of my paralytic embrace with the floor, I lurched to my feet and clump-padded to the kitchen, one shoe off and one shoe on like Diddle, Diddle Dumpling.

I ripped open the refrigerator door only to find an agonizing hollow. A wasteland. A barren tundra. Empty! The magnitude of this bleakness held me in place like iron filings in a magnetic field. A huge effort was necessary to break free by slamming the door.

A light winked in my head.

The freezer! Of course, the freezer. The beautiful, life-sustaining freezer. I had been cramming it against a time of need. For example, I might be bedridden and abandoned, and this stash could save me (although how I'd use it bedridden and abandoned was unclear). Or I might be dead broke; then the cache would be a lifesaver. (Although how I'd pay the rent that housed me as well as the freezer was unclear.) Or I might be in the throes of creating the Great American Lyric Drama and have no time to waste on marketing or restaurant outings. (Although how I'd save time by defrosting, cooking and dishwashing was unclear.)

But now was a clear time of need. The freezer was about to pay its freight. I gimped back to the bedroom, which garaged it.

Standing in front of my double-door, extra-cubic-foot-capacity job, I paused a moment to enjoy its majestic appearance before slowly opening the doors, parting them like a theater curtain to reveal an exotic stage setting. Meticulous care was necessary because it was packed beyond its capacity. Many a time my midnight marauding for ice cream had resulted in a frozen matzoh ball finding a vulnerable toe.

For a moment, I simply looked with hungry eyes at my overflowing cornucopia. After an enchanting inspection, I felt a twinge of irritation. It was time to make a choice. The beckoning ice cream and chocolate cake I rejected out of hand because I intended to have them for dessert. After all I'd been through, I meant to make a meal of it.

Roasts and fowl, had they even been defrosted, would take too much time to fix. I narrowed the possibilities to a variety of TV dinners or the mess of broiling a frozen steak.

I kicked off my remaining shoe and flailed the air with my other foot, forgetting that that shoe was already off. When I finally realized my foot was unshod, I cursed a malicious fate for trying to make a fool of me. Calm was restored as I felt myself drawn back to the steak. I removed a seven-pound sirloin without causing a ripple elsewhere. The two-inch thickness sent a thrilling message to my salivary glands. I swallowed. In the pause, I was stricken with a momentary doubt. This monster would take more than a bit of broiling. However, my anticipation of the juicy results won the day. And speed, at the moment, wasn't critical. It could cook while I soaked in a warm tub.

I placed the frozen dinosaur slab in the broiler, which I set at 500 degrees. I took care to switch on the exhaust fan, anticipating a bit of smoke. My joy was so complete that I rewarded myself with a pint of chocolate chip ice cream to kind of enhance my tub.

Upon leaving the bath, I was instantly aware that something was wrong. The entire apartment was thick with a fatty layer of smog that almost obscured the lights. But my keen sense of smell told me it wasn't a real fire. It was only the steak.

Only the steak! Oh, my God!

I made a dash for the kitchen.

The walls were black with oily soot, the broiler engulfed in an inferno. Unpleasant sizzling noises came from all directions as bubbles of beef fat exploded like fragmentation shells.

I grabbed a twin-pronged serving fork and lunged heroically at the incendiary steak. But fate chose this moment to reveal to me the true nature of paradox. Only one-quarter inch of the slab of meat was on fire. The rest was still frozen solid. I was witnessing the phenomenon of flaming ice. Broiler versus freezer.

However exotic this display of modern science beating hell out of itself might be, I had no other thought than to save my endangered steak. Repeated jabs with the needle-sharp tines were as fruitless as chopping at a glacier with a rubber ice pick. Throwing the utensil aside, I clawed wildly through a drawer until I found a pair of tongs.

I finally grasped the blazing beef and rescued it. For my pains, the sizzling beast spat in my face. Howling, I dropped it. The kitchen floor erupted, looking like a vinyl-tiled barbecue pit. I grabbed a dish towel and smothered the flames.

With admirable presence of mind, I doused the residual fire in the broiler and turned off the heat. Removing the towel from the steak, I observed the scorched surface, under which lay something about as digestible as a prehistoric specimen just uncovered on the Siberian steppe.

I inspected the side that had been on the floor. It didn't look good.

But having come this far, I couldn't give up. Turning on the hot water tap, I doggedly washed away the grit and replaced it on the broiler. It hissed like a den of cobras.

Switching the temperature to a moderate 250 degrees, I was aware of a depressing wait before that steak would be edible. But as I needed to bathe again, I thought things might work out.

Spotting the serving fork on the floor, I was seized by fury at its ineptitude. The ungrateful son of a bitch had been taking up drawer space for God knows how long. I hurled it against the wall. Instead of the satisfying Jim Bowie effect, it sounded off a sickly boing-

boing and dropped behind the stove. My only satisfaction was that maybe I speared a mouse.

Heading back to the tub, I reflected on my new problem. Time was now of the reverse essence. I had an overabundance to kill. What to do?

Since this would be an extended bath, why not do it right? I brightened and gathered together a quart of rocky road ice cream and a box of frozen brownies. Placing these upon a little side table near the tub, I was struck that it still lacked a little something. I fished in a bookshelf for a copy of the *Kama Sutra* and settled into my bath to enjoy a little piece of New York on the Ganges, where East meets West.

I lay back in the tub and nibbled and read and sweated more than usual. Although I owned up to a mild scorn for Far Eastern sexual rituals, I had underestimated the effect of the *Kama Sutra*. I had also underestimated the amount of time it would take to become waterlogged. With a great effort, I forced myself out of the tub and began toweling my water-scrunched skin.

A cinder, possibly from my four-alarm scullery fire, wandered into my left eye. Wrapping the towel around my middle, I peered into the medicine cabinet mirror to inspect it. Before I could get a close look, the towel slipped and fell off. I picked it up, rewrapped myself and again put my face up to the mirror. Again the towel slipped off.

My girth made it impossible to wrap the bath towel securely around me. There was too little terry cloth to tuck in after just once around my circumference. Such a nasty bit of exposure, coming in the midst of all my troubles, was not pleasant to contemplate. I barely avoided a ruined evening by the timely return of my appetite. By now, the steak should have broiled to a mouth-watering turn.

My spirits lightened as I trundled toward the kitchen.

At the threshold, I popped my head in for a quick look-see. No smoke, no flame, no fumes, I noted smugly. On to the steak. Removing it to a platter, I picked up a sharply honed carving knife and made the critical test cut and taste.

Were it an American ritual, I most certainly would have performed Hara Kiri. The charred surface of my steak concealed a raw purple beneath, leading to a center that had barely thawed and was cold as ice.

The temptation to panic was barely short of overwhelming. Yet I exhibited a decisiveness in adversity only given to a chosen few in the annals of conflict. I committed my strategic reserve.

Rudy's Delicatessen sported a sign that covered half the storefront. A mixture of Gothic and Gay Nineties curlicue-style lettering proclaimed:

OPEN ALL NIGHT
AND ALSO 24 HOURS FOR YOUR CONVENIENCE.

WE DELIVER ALL NIGHT
AND ALSO 24 HOURS
(*Except for Yom Kippur we are strictly closed.*)

RUDY SAYS:
WHY TRY TO SLEEP
ON AN EMPTY BELLY?

JUST CALL RUDY'S ALL-NIGHT AND ALSO 24-HOUR DELI.

A call to this savior of long standing would quickly produce an appetizer while I waited for the steak to submit. I dialed.

"Rudy's all-night and twenty-four-hour deli."

"Hi, Rudy. I need fast . . ."

"Mr. Greene! You been a stranger since you got so skinny. Boy oh boy! Your loss was my loss. But look out you shouldn't get sick!"

Rudy never forgot a face or a voice. And he was as famous for his repartee as he was for his great pastrami. But at the moment, his well-meaning heartiness threatened him with the loss of a paying customer.

"Rudy. I'm in a big rush."

"That's show business, Mr. Greene. I should know. I don't sing and dance, but I gotta show up with the goods on time too. And no stand-in stuff from the Stage Deli or my audience will know on the first bite."

"Rudy," I grated, "no philosophy. I said I'm in a rush. Now I need . . ."

"O.K., O.K. I'm coming. So what happened? A bunch dropped in on you and since you became a scarecrow you got nothing to eat in the house to give them. Am I right?"

Rudy unwittingly, or perhaps very shrewdly, had provided me with an excuse for a large order.

"Right as usual, Rudy. A half a pound of chopped liver. Wait. Make that a whole pound. My friends look like a pack of hungry wolves. Three double-decker pastrami sandwiches, a couple of pints of potato salad, a dozen dill pickles and a case of Coke. Got that, Rudy?"

"Only three pastramis for the bunch? Maybe you should take a pound on the side in case somebody wants more. And also more bread."

"O.K. Rudy, will this be delivered in the usual fifteen minutes?" This had been our mutual understanding in the past and Rudy always came through.

"A few minutes more or less, Mr. Greene. Give them all to drink. They won't even notice."

I didn't like the sound of that. With the trauma of the steak still fresh and a nerve-shattering wait ahead of me, I was in desperate need.

"Rudy," I said menacingly, "my guests are hungry. Very hungry. No few minutes more or less. The usual fifteen minutes or else."

"Mr. Greene, I'll be honest with you. The boy just went out with two orders. But the minute he's back, he comes right to you. O.K.?"

"Not O.K. Fifteen minutes or else I call Looey's. He's not that far away."

"You want to poison your friends?"

"Rudy!" I barked, completely blowing my cool.

"I'll send it with the chef. Don't worry. It's on its way already."

"Fifteen minutes, Rudy."

I hung around the kitchen just staring at the steak. As each little crackle announced a surface bead of fat exploding, I almost cheered. I counted 132 pops in fifteen minutes. No Rudy. After two minutes' grace, I counted fourteen more. But still no Rudy. I grabbed the phone.

"Rudy's all-night . . ."

"Where is it, Rudy?"

"You mean to say the chef didn't deliver yet, Mr. Greene?"

"No, Rudy, where is it?"

"I'll give him hell, don't worry, Mr. Greene."

"Rudy," I said, "if the stuff isn't delivered in exactly five minutes, you can shove it where it'll make no profit."

"Wait, wait. I think I hear the delivery boy coming back and . . ."

I slammed down the phone. Why tell me about the return of the delivery boy if the chef had been sent out in the first place? I hunched over the phone, watching the clock. If the order didn't arrive in exactly five minutes, Looey would get my business.

Five minutes later, I called this alternate back-up system and repeated the order. Out of spite, I added a few bagel-lox-cream-cheese-and-onion combinations.

Before I could think of a way to murder Rudy and pin it on Looey, the bell rang. I started for the door but changed course to get into a robe. Returning to the threshold, I realized that I needed cash because this would be my first transaction with Looey. While I was thundering back to the bedroom the bell rang again, causing me a near header as I tripped over one of my fallen shoes. I was livid.

"What's the goddam rush?" I yelled. "I'm coming."

I opened the door and was confronted by two delivery boys.

"Looey's," said one.

"Rudy's," said the other.

Looey's guy was first. Holding out a monstrously

stuffed paper sack, he said: "That'll be twenty-seven dollars and sixty-three cents."

I took the package but couldn't very well dig into my wallet at the same time, so I thrust it back to the boy. Pulling a twenty and a ten, we exchanged money and package while he made change. Or more precisely, a sprinkling of pennies, nickels and dimes plus the two bills hit the floor: a splendid display of the delivery kid's art of tip pyramiding. I knew he'd take an hour recovering the money, so I said:

"Hey kid, just keep all of it."

"Thanks," he replied, and retrieved every cent in one clean sweep.

During all of this, Rudy's boy waited patiently. As I was about to back off and shut the door, he smiled pleasantly and thrust his load at me.

"Rudy says this one's on the house. And also he gave me the tip."

Too surprised to react at this turn of events, I embraced the new burden and staggered into the kitchen. The boy pulled the door shut as I dropped the stuff on the table. At that instant, the unpredictable steak flared up in flames again.

But being at the scene of the outbreak made a difference. I did the fireman routine with calm efficiency. After all, with two back-up systems Go, the absolute stake of my steak was no longer absolute.

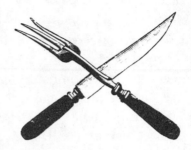

settled comfortably onto my bed, flanked by two night tables, each bristling with a stuffed paper sack. On a little cocktail table stood a huge bucket of ice, twelve Cokes, and two oversized tumblers, souvenirs of a divorce settlement.

Before starting my feast, I picked up *TV Guide*. At 2:30 A.M., I had a choice of several old movie goodies and I lingered a bit before deciding in order to hone an already razor-edged anticipation. Just as I was about to turn on the set, I had a thought: From now on, nothing must interfere with my hard-won spoils. I called my answering service, instructing the sleepy-voiced girl to pick up on the first ring and that no matter what emergency was claimed by no matter who, I was out of town indefinitely. Her "Yes, sir," "Certainly, sir," betrayed some incredulity about phone traffic at such an hour.

I clicked on the TV remote and filled both glasses with ice and Coke. Reaching into either sack, I hauled out a couple of sandwiches. "Move over, Heaven," I said, "here I come."

A fusillade of shots from a vintage horse opera accompanied my first bite into a pastrami sandwich. The sensation defied description.

I chewed, swallowed and drank with a speed and gusto that matched the wild action on the screen. At the height of the battle, the picture abruptly cut to an endless array of tombstones.

An authoritative voice intoned solemnly: "Many roads lead to Rome." The camera pulled back to reveal a sign: Cemetery of Rome, New York. Then came a quick cut to a man at a banquet table. Speeded-up, jerky movements and distorted angles showed him gobbling obscenely. A fast zoom-in froze on his blurred, agonized face as he clutched his chest and keeled over. The voice-over intoned, "The Surgeon General of the United States warns you against taking this road."

I clicked over to another channel.

"When you eat too well, demand Di-Gel," advised a rhyming goon.

I turned off the sound. Why the hell was such garbage allowed on the air, I wondered while I fished out more sandwiches from my paper larders.

Meanwhile, back to my horse opera and the battle of Little Big Horn. The war whooping, hoof thundering, bullet whining intensified . . . and climaxed with the Ayd's Reducing Plan.

I switched channels.

A blazing tank battle in the African desert was kicking up a storm of sand. Nodding approval, I tore into another sandwich and chewed excitedly. But the food turned cold in my mouth as this channel went from the ridiculous to the insulting by spewing out *its* load of commercials, starting with a Get-in-Shape-America Spa. The virtues of beautiful slenderhood sneered at the vices of ugly obesity. And promised lots of vigorous virility instead of that old flabby impotence.

I flicked from channel to channel in growing disbelief as I passed through feeling lousy with Bromo, joining the Diet-Pepsi generation, glowing with health through a Grapenuts breakfast that filled me up, not out, and jogged through the rain to keep in shape, but was cautioned to eat aspirin like mad. When at last the vicious assault was over, I was a badly shaken man. There was nothing in my contract with the Government that said my taxes, which supported the FCC, would be used to underwrite the disruption of my pleasures by granting broadcast franchises to the crummy TV networks.

The tank action blazed up spectacularly and diverted me. I reached into a paper sack and chewed away with renewed absorption. I got a little itchy because I hadn't seen the end of the horse opera, but I couldn't tear myself away from Rommel's panzers and Montgomery's artillery.

I noted with malicious satisfaction that the new sandwich I was eating came from Looey's side of the bed and tasted a hell of a lot better than Rudy's. There was no comparison between the two pastramis.

Sparing a moment from the fiery barrel of an 88, I turned an appreciative eye on Looey's merchandise. It didn't look right. Although my left hand held a half-eaten pastrami sandwich, my right hand was gooey with cream cheese as it clutched the remaining fragment of a bagel and lox.

This discovery stopped me cold because no matter how you slice them, lox and pastrami will never make a mixed grill. Never.

I made a command decision: I'd save whatever remained of these appetizers for tomorrow. And besides, the steak had to be done by now.

I picked up my two paper sacks and returned to the kitchen, a little worried that I couldn't tell the difference between lox and pastrami. I wondered whether my taste buds were jaded. Or was this merely the result of overconcentrating on the TV? The sight of the broiler wrested my attention from further speculation. I noted with pride how orderly everything was. There was no smoke, no flame, no splattering. As I looked closer, I discovered there was also no heat. Then I remembered: When the steak flared up the last time, I had turned the broiler off.

That tore it. I had a tantrum. Why was I picked out, after billions of years of evolution and thousands of years of history, to be brought to the very point of madness on this night? What cosmic forces assigned so evil a star to preside over my destiny? Of all the sparkling beauties that gently tacked the night in against the sky, why did I have the only malevolent one in the firmament, ready to nail me at every turn?

A couple of tears spurted from my eyes. Throwing the paper sacks to the floor, I stomped on them like a wild animal. A pickle squirted out. I kicked viciously at it, but merely grazed its end. It made two soggy revolutions and stopped dead.

I looked at the steak. How does a mere hunk of beef die twice? Once at the slaughterhouse and once in a stinking hot and cold broiler, that's how. I began a desperate search of the cupboards, not really knowing what I was looking for. Then my eye lit on a few cans of soup. An idea formed. If the steak wouldn't come with heat to me, I would come with heat to it. I'd simply fire up some sauce and scald the son of a bitch!

But soup was too thin. I needed a rich sauce, too thick to boil. It had to bubble like molten lava. Among an assortment of thick sauces, I chose the largest can and opened it. After a split second's hesitation, I put the can right on the burner. Why louse up a pot?

While it was heating, I wrangled the lifeless steak onto the platter. Then I poured half a bottle of heavy catsup over it; the rest I unthinkingly poured into the heating sauce. Splash, sizzle, bloody mess. I forgot that the sauce was brimful in its can. I restrained the terrible urge to throw the offending catsup bottle to the floor. Bare feet on catsup-colored glass wouldn't even show the blood, so why go to the trouble?

When the sauce was puff-puffing I dumped it on the steak, can and all. To insure against any further frustration, I piled the carving knife and a fork on top of the heap and hefted the platter. Jesus! It weighed a ton. Laboring to the bedroom, I spotted the label on the sauce can. Chocolate Fudge. But I carried on rather casually. After all, it was hot. And that was the object. Besides, nobody ever tried molten fudge on steak. This could be the start of a cattleman's baked Alaska.

I made the bedroom in time to see the tail end of a

commercial about the Roman Meal Diet Plan. "Drop dead," I yelled at the set. On cue, the Nazis were back at their old artillery and bombing games.

I cut into the steak and stuffed a hefty chunk into my maw. The boiling hot fudge raised a blister on the roof of my mouth. The catsup was neutral. The steak was rough-charred on the surface and very chilly in the center. So I couldn't really decide about the overall taste of this combination. After another bite, I felt an overwhelming need for sleep. Besides, I had to admit I wasn't ravenous any more. A little snooze might do me good.

I simply put the platter down on the floor next to the bed. A hell of a feat of balance, all things considered. I clicked off the German version of *The Desert Song* and shut my eyes.

In the blackness of sleep, I followed my own image: There I was, a soldier, wandering across a desert sown with mines. Suddenly, my own battalion let loose a furious artillery barrage. With no foxhole to dive into, and the terrifying knowledge that to hit the dirt was a sure way to trigger a mine, I froze. The slim chance I had for survival was to crouch as low as possible without moving a muscle.

I cried out, hoping the sound of my voice would wake me up. A familiar voice responded.

"You called?"

Skinny was back. I was hysterically grateful. But too soon. I was still a stationary target, crouching so low, my muscles were fairly singing in tension.

"Pretty tight fix you're in, Fatso," he said pleasantly.

"Get me out of this," I whispered fiercely.

"You'll have to speak up if I'm to hear you through this racket, Fatso."

"Go to hell," I answered bitterly.

"From the looks of things around here, I'd say we're pretty close."

There was a moment of dead silence. Then I was almost knocked off my feet as Skinny's voice boomed like the artillery.

"You are a slobbering, fat, greedy, grabby, blubbery slob."

"That's a lie. I have an undiagnosed glandular condition."

"*Cop-out*," Skinny boomed. "You've passed more tests than a rocket to the moon."

"But a man needs to eat to stay alive."

"*Cop-out*. You don't eat like a man. You eat like a pig."

I squealed in protest.

"I had a deprived childhood. Eating is my only compensation."

"*Cop-out*. That's a lousy compensation! Plenty of people buck backgrounds like that. But they become athletes, scholars or models."

"I just haven't exercised my willpower yet."

"*Cop-out*. Your willpower is legend. It stretches all the way from your hand to your mouth."

"Wait a minute. I read all about that. An unconscious compulsion can't be affected by willpower. That's a basic law of psychology."

"*Cop-out*. What about all those people who've broken that law? Ex-nail biters, ex-drinkers, ex-junkies and ex-fatsos. You are a coward. You are a weakling. You've never really tried."

I blazed back.

"What! I've tried Ayds, yoga, hypnosis. I've tried low-fat high-protein diets, low-protein and no-fat diets, all-protein no-carbohydrates diets, fruit diets, rice diets, banana diets, rabbit-food diets. I've tried a lot."

"*Cop-out*. You've never tried not eating."

"Food is like sex to me. I can't give it up."

"*Cop-out*. You are sexless. You are roundly, profoundly sexless. You stand for sex repeal. When was the last time you could see past your gut? For all you know, you may be a eunuch."

This was hitting below the belt.

"You're crazy. A person doesn't have to see to know."

"*Cop-out*. The truth is: Out of sight, out of mind, out of business."

"Sex isn't the only thing in life. I've got friends. Lots of friends!"

"*Cop-out*. You don't have any real friends."

"That's a lie. Lots of people would be sorry to see me die."

"Sure. Swift's, Armour's, Howard Johnson's and Charlie the Tuna."

At this unkindest cut of all, I cried out in pain. My leg muscles, frozen in that crouch, were in spasm. I flailed the air trying to maintain my balance. But in vain. As I hit the ground, a mine exploded under my chest.

Next morning, I would have heaved a sigh of relief that I was alive, had I been able to breathe freely.

Any attempt to draw a deep breath was cut short by an invisible pair of front and rear walls that seemed to tighten like a vise, causing a generalized, but none-theless exquisite pain. I speculated with growing fear, which took only a second to become a certainty, that I had suffered a severe heart attack.

I knew I should call my doctor, but two obstacles barred the way. First, I felt too rotten to move. Second, I was convinced that when my diagnosis of a heart attack was confirmed, I'd immediately suffer another and final one. Yet I couldn't lie there, immobi-lized, until discovered by the buzzards overhead.

I bypassed these grizzly thoughts by concentrating on moving my fingers and toes. And went through an elaborate process, the reverse of which was commonly recommended for sleep. Activating all my ambulatory muscles, I moved, tensed and held them at readiness until I could mobilize enough component parts of my anatomy to crank myself to a sitting position. I sweated pails before I could swing my legs over the edge of the bed, only to have my feet touch the cold, sticky mess of fudge, catsup and limp steak.

The shock caused a sudden intake of breath that crumbled the walls around my chest to a mound of gravel. I could almost see the dust rising inside my guts. I coughed painfully. Then I panicked. How much more of this could my damaged heart take before it conked out?

The ring of the phone startled me. My heart pounded. The service picked up in the middle of the third ring and I eavesdropped.

"Mr. Greene's residence."

"Oh, uh, well . . ."

"Who's calling, please?"

"Carolyn Jones. Did he leave any message?"

"Mr. Greene is out of town indefinitely, Miss Jones."

"Out of town, but that's . . . but I spoke with him late last night."

"I'm sorry, Miss Jones, I'm the day operator. The instructions are that Mr. Greene is out of town. May I take a message?"

"Well, just tell him I called."

"Thank you, Miss Jones. Goodbye."

Click, click, click, went three hangups. I flushed, ashamed. Carolyn sounded so bewildered. Why hadn't I answered her? Because I'm too sick, I lied to myself. And quickly twisted the lie to that most suspect of human virtues: nobility. Why should I worry her with my troubles?

Oh Christ! The answering service operator! She had to know I was listening in. My sickness took a turn for the worse. I could see the blind item in the gossip columns. "What TV star, now on a national tour, has been calling what Broadway conductor and getting that old 'out of town' reprise from his answering service?"

The pile of gravel inside my guts rumbled ominously and loosened my anxiety and self-pity. I picked up the phone and called my doctor.

"Well, what seems to be the trouble, Herb?"

"I feel played out, Frank. Every time I try a deep breath, my coccyx bone rattles."

"Are you having chest pains along with the breathing problems?"

That he spotted this over the phone scared the hell out of me. If I told him the truth, Frank would send an ambulance. No need to prejudice his judgment up front, I thought.

"No, I don't think so. I mean, it's nothing local. Just a general collapse."

"Look, grab a cab and come over. I just had a cancellation and it can't hurt to take a look."

A couple of hours later, I was back home. Frank's words were still ringing in my ears.

"Get rid of that weight and stop turning your digestive system into a sewage treatment plant. And go back to your walks. Remember your legs. Your muscle tone couldn't compete with last week's jello."

My relief over having escaped a heart attack was so

great that I suffered no embarrassment at this dressing down. Quite the contrary, I rather welcomed it. But in a little while I began having my doubts and suspicions. What if Frank muffed this one? What if he missed the one tiny symptom that, if recognized in time, could save my life? Such things were not unknown. It wasn't long before my agitation worked up to the profound conviction that my savage heart attack had been misdiagnosed as a simple bellyache.

I want another opinion, I decided as I counted my pulse. I saw another doctor the next day. And on the following morning, a third.

Diagnosis: obesity caused by excessive food intake.

Treatment: weight reduction by rigorous restriction of the cause.

I left the last consulting room and waddled along aimlessly. Up this street, down the other, oblivious to my surroundings. Just following my nose. And soon found myself in the midst of a hundred food smells. Wherever I turned, with every step, the aroma and sight of food rocked me. Saliva squirted into my mouth, causing a mixed pain-pleasure. My tongue went into spasm as I pressed my nose against the window of a huge delicatessen. I almost swooned at the sight of the steaming corned beef, the spiced pastrami and the profusion of other cholesterol banks.

Tearing myself away, I lurched down the street only to become glued to the windowpane of the most lavish pastry shop in the city. The curling rivers of whipped cream ran in heartbreaking, luscious designs, topping an endless variety of puffs, tortes, éclairs and layered beauties. I almost sucked my teeth from their sockets.

Compared with this caloric hell, Dante's Inferno was a health spa. Food shop upon food shop, supermarkets overflowing to the street, elegant bistros and proletarian hamburger joints alike, all combined to produce a glittering nightmare. I took it until my legs turned to jelly. Just in time, I found a nearby street lamp for support.

Breathing heavily, I heard myself rasp, "I'm a foodaholic, that's what I am, a good-for-nothing, low-life, goddamn foodaholic."

A woman and young child passed. I heard the mother say, "Pay no attention, Terry dear, he's drunk."

Another passerby stumbled toward me. His legs stopped, but his body continued forward in an uncoordinated sway. He winked owlishly. " 'S right on, man. 'S right on."

A cab pulled up and discharged a fare. I almost knocked a wizened old man off his feet in my hysteria to be gone.

"You must be in a hurry, bud. Where to?" the driver asked.

I mumbled my address.

"So what's up there that's so important you almost knocked off that old geezer? Jesus H! Everybody can't wait to get home and fight with the old lady or drop dead."

decided it was time to take stock of things. A kind of personal inventory.

With pencil and paper in hand, I managed to list a few things I was wrecking.

Carolyn
Work
Carolyn
Morale
Carolyn
Health
Carolyn
Looks
Carolyn

I couldn't get beyond these because I could see a huge tome expanding like a telephone directory, whose every item had my number.

In sheer exasperation, I spoke aloud.

"All right, come on out, you skinny son of a bitch."

I waited.

Nothing.

"You only show up when you want," I reproached him bitterly. "Where the hell are you when I want?"

"Cool it, Fatso, I've been here all the time. But you nearly killed me with your last dose of nourishment."

"I apologize. Honest. I only wanted to get out of my lousy mood. Look, Skinny, I need your help. Because, man, I'm licked."

"I'm always ready to help, Fatso. Now, what's your most aggravating problem about being fat?"

"That's easy. I'm always hungry."

"You? Hungry? Come on, Fatso, no dumb put-ons. That's like saying a drunk is always thirsty. How could you know the first thing about being hungry when you never feel full?"

"You're right of course. Funny I never thought of it that way before. It sounds insane that I eat so much when I'm not hungry."

"What do you mean, sounds insane? It is insane."

"So where do we go from here?"

"Right back to the beginning. And think before you answer. What's your most aggravating problem about being fat?"

I thought about it. It didn't take long.

"I'm embarrassed at the way I look."

"You mean, of course, you're afraid that you turn women off sexually?"

"Yes."

"And specifically, Carolyn?"

"Yes."

"Why hasn't that been enough of a motive to lose the weight?"

"I don't know."

"Is it possible you don't really want that relationship?"

"But I want to marry Carolyn."

"But you feel that your obesity may kill what you want. So you want and don't want at the same time."

"That sounds like a stale choice from a tired psychoanalytic menu."

"It is, Fatso, it is."

"Then why are you pushing it? I've been psychoanalyzed black, blue and broke. And look at me. Those bastards told me I'm well adjusted professionally and I don't hate my mother. But my sexual functioning was an illusion. I was waiting to get impotent so they could have something to cure. They didn't help me. They just made me get fatter."

"No, Fatso. You're the one who ate like a horse, so why blame a bunch of jackasses for becoming the jolly Herbert Greene giant?"

"They could have been honest, at least."

"Honest? Don't be fatheaded too, heavy man. How would their honesty have affected your gluttony?"

"I'd have looked for someone who understood the problem, that's how."

"My stomach is too delicate to swallow mother's milk, let alone your burnt offerings. Goodbye."

"Wait! You said you'd help me."

"All right, all right. But let's simplify things. As I see it, you have several choices. The statistics show that diets are not for fat people, since less than two percent ever stay thin. So your first choice is to eat, drink and be merry, for tomorrow you may die."

"You call that help? I just told you I'm not merry with that routine. I'm miserable."

"I didn't finish, Fatso. I know you're not merry. Therefore, commit suicide."

"What? You can't be serious."

"Stop interrupting. That's simply another choice. There are more. For instance: Regard your fat trouble as a natural handicap like a gimpy leg or a split palate. That would take the pressure off. You don't judge a cripple or a defective for something he can't help. So stop judging yourself."

"But I can't stop others from judging me."

"True. But you've lived with that for a long time. And we both know you're not shy about defending yourself."

"But I don't like to do that. People say I'm a heartless louse."

"Tough. Another choice is to admit you are weak and have no will to act. After all, everybody has a cross to bear. Yours happens to be fat."

My heart sank. Every one of Skinny's choices stuck in my craw. In desperation, I howled.

"You bastard! You're worse than a grave robber. You want to rob me of hope!"

"Hope? Don't be a schmuck. I wouldn't even rob you of illusions, let alone hope."

"What the hell do you call what you've been doing, you torpedo?"

"Trying to get you to fight. Where there's fight,

there's life. And where there's life, there's hope. You're suffering delusions, and those things are dangerous to mess with. Relax, let's break out some Scotch. I'll buy you a drink."

"You know something? I don't really like you."

"Why should you? After all, you invented me."

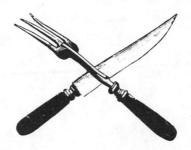

Although never a devout believer in do-it-yourself amateurs doing it to themselves, my encounter with Skinny exposed this attitude as prejudice. I had to admit to the tingle of hope I felt as a result of his visit. Next to love, hope is the most irresistible force. Even to a seemingly immovable object such as my obesity. I decided to fight.

So I headed for Brentano's. The number of hardbacks, paperbacks, booklets, pamphlets and pocket-size publications on the subject of obesity was staggering. I was rattled by the variety of approaches and had no way of judging which was good, better, best.

At the height of my bewilderment, a plump girl came by and deliberately chose a book from the shelf. As she opened it, I glimpsed the ripping energy of its title: *It's Crazy, Suicidal and Unnecessary to Be Fat,* by Arnold Godwin, M.D. I could barely wait until she moved away in order to get a copy of my own. Something in that title grabbed me: its truth. The back of the dust jacket made the sale without any further examination. It asked:

> *Do you eat when you're not hungry?*
> *Are you a solitary eater?*
> *Do you eat whether you're happy, depressed or simply bored?*
> *Have you failed miserably at every attempt to diet?*

The questions were followed by an attractive bit of boldness.

The answers are obvious. Otherwise you wouldn't be reading this. If you want to change your life completely, read this book and stop fooling around.

I flashed money, made tracks and was barely settled in my chair before I began devouring the book. It divided into three sections: a discussion of the dynamics of obesity and its treatment, a sampling of case histories and last a huge thesaurus of reducing and maintenance diets. As a postscript, there followed an exhaustive list of foods, foreign and domestic, along with their caloric values.

The main thrust of the book lay in its practical approach to the problem: immediate action in helping those afflicted. Its modesty and warmth were apparent and disarming. The author admitted at the outset: "The cause and cure of obesity are still to be discovered. But we've come a long way in the relatively short time since the problem has become defined as a very serious threat to the well-being of more than 50 percent of Americans."

With this unpretentious, pragmatic view, Dr. Godwin outlined a number of theories that most authorities agreed upon. While not absolutely committing himself, he appeared to incline more toward a permissive rather than an authoritarian point of view.

He considered it "vital to avoid adding to the dieter's torment" and went to great lengths in devising the "greatest variety and quantity of food consistent with weight loss or maintenance." He was most emphatic that "restriction should never be confused with deprivation and discomfort. In twenty-five years of clinical experience, I've seen too many dieters founder on just such treacherous shoals.

"A diet that torments the dieter with constant pangs of hunger is not only unnecessarily cruel and punishing, but sooner or later causes increasing irritability leading to rebellion. And what can be a more healthy sign in a person than to rebel furiously at being tortured every day of his life?"

After reading through some touching and impressive case histories, I felt much more than hope. I felt certainty. This was what I'd been searching for. The book confirmed and reconfirmed this confidence as I easily spotted myself in the letters that appeared at the end of each case history. I memorized a few pithy quotes:

From an economist: "I have discovered the one economic law that has no exceptions: Obesity is a form of conspicuous consumption common only to those least able to afford it. It bankrupts every system without fail."

From an insurance executive: "Our actuarial tables show the old notion that death plays no favorites to be a myth. It sometimes postpones itself for thin people."

From a minister: "It makes one shiver to imagine the damage to Christianity had the Lord weighed 450 pounds. Such a thing might have broken the faith, bang right on the cross."

That Dr. Godwin had treated some pretty extraordinary people seemed clear from the sampling of letters he printed. That Dr. Godwin was a pretty extraordinary man himself appeared self-evident. That I wanted to become a member of his club was certain.

Why not find the man himself rather than attempt a do-it-yourself thing from the text? I grabbed the Manhattan phone book and prayed that he was a New Yorker. And prayed harder that if so, he was listed. And intensified my prayers that if he was a New Yorker and if he was listed in the directory, he was still practicing.

Jackpot time! This being Friday, I got an appointment Monday at 11:00 A.M. If what I'd felt upon reading the book had been euphoria, now I was in orbit. I dipped into the most pleasing passages repeatedly, and tried conjuring up what Dr. Godwin looked like. But whether he appeared tall or short, forty or fifty, he always looked wiry, spare, possessed of mischievous eyes that gazed upon the human scene with ironic tolerance. I finally resolved my image to a forty-three-year-old man, 5 feet 11 inches tall, with steel-blue-gray hair, dancing blue eyes, 150 pounds of tempered flesh and bone, dressed in elegant tweeds that he wore as casually and gracefully as a cat wears its coat.

I took the book to bed and before I knew it, I fell fast asleep. It was 7:30 A.M. when I awakened, exactly eleven hours after I'd conked out. I rolled out of bed, showered and had some black coffee. By God, I thought, brimming with goodwill and joy, I've got to tell somebody about this or bust. Then I cautioned myself: cool it, don't put a hex on it. So I compromised. I'd say something to somebody, O.K., but I didn't have to go into the details.

Carolyn! Yes, Carolyn, of course, Carolyn. Who else but Carolyn? Besides, I owed her an explanation for that answering-service thing. San Francisco, here I call, I hummed as I dialed through. A few toots, squawks, beeps and whines later and I heard the reassuring ring of the phone at the Mark Hopkins.

"Miss Jones? One moment, please."

Then a crackly voice answered.

"Yes, hello?"

"Carolyn? Carolyn! The greatest thing in the world has happened. I just don't know how to describe it."

"What time is it?"

"Time? Oh, let's see. Eight fifteen."

She groaned.

"Not here, it's not. It's five fifteen and I have a matinee today and oh, hell. Did you just get back from out of town? How are you?"

I clattered on. "No, I didn't."

"Didn't what?"

"Just get back. I haven't been away anywhere to get back from."

"But your service said . . ."

"Oh well, that's a long story and I can't wait. I mean, I'm bursting. You couldn't possibly guess what's happened. You'd never guess in a lifetime."

"I won't even try. What is it, a new show?"

"Well, actually, I can't really tell you. It's a surprise."

"Herbert Greene, if you're still smashed, I'll kill you."

"Me? Oh no. I'm sober, honest. I'm just up, excited. Anyway, will you marry me?"

"What?"

"I said, will you marry me?"

"Darling, that's a beautiful surprise."

"No. That's not the surprise. That's for after the surprise."

There was a pause.

"Hello? Carolyn? You still there?"

"I'm not sure. I'm a little confused . . ."

"I'm sorry, darling. Look, you go back to sleep now. After all, you've got two shows today. I just had to let off some steam."

"But . . ."

"No, no. Not another word. Go back to sleep and rest," I said firmly. And hung up.

The phone rang.

"Hello?"

"Did you just call and ask me to marry you?"

"Carolyn? Darling, now come on, you promised you'd go back to sleep," and again I hung up with noble resolution.

Monday it rained. My first thought was for the safety of Dr. Godwin. Manhattan traffic in the rain is not without its risks. Dr. Godwin might have to subdue a half-dozen weather-maddened New Yorkers before he ever reached his office. And with Dr. Godwin booked for assault and all, where would that leave me?

The phone rang. It was Dr. Godwin's office calling to confirm my appointment. The crisp efficiency of this procedure thrilled me and strengthened the feeling that I might soon be calling the doctor God for short as well as for long.

Exactly between the fifth and sixth peals of the local deacon's eleven o'clock church chimes, I rang the doctor's bell. The eleventh-hour echo was minutes into history before I noticed the instructions on the door below Dr. Godwin's name: Don't ring bell. Walk in.

I opened the door and stepped into the reception room. Four thousand pounds of people were anchored in six chairs. I took the only remaining seat and cast a furtive eye around. Those not pretending to leaf through the usual reception room literature were casting not-so-furtive eyes back at me. I got a flash as to why: I had at least a 150-pound drop on anybody in the joint. I began to feel guilty I wasn't in the elephant class. I noticed a pair of hippos exchange mean looks and then jerk their heads my way.

Desperate, I blurted in the direction of the hostile hippos, "Dr. Godwin is a magician. I've lost one hundred and fifty pounds already. He's a wonder."

That did the trick. The whole room was suddenly flooded in a friendly togetherness sweat, the result of the mass effort of blubber-laden jowls to smile. A few minutes passed less disagreeably. Then I noticed a funny thing. The faces in the reception room changed, but the body count remained the same. Like traffic in a cafeteria at lunchtime, one body entered the inner office and was replaced by the arrival of another meat mountain. Instead of the extended wait I anticipated, scarcely fifteen minutes elapsed before I was ushered into the examining room.

I was greeted by a medium-sized man of medium weight, wearing a medium mustache and looking a medium forty-five years of age. His handshake was medium strong and his voice a medium-soft medium baritone.

"Mr. Greene, I am Arnold Godwin."

I had no chance to evaluate my reactions because Dr. Godwin displayed an office routine that, for sheer unrushed but dazzling efficiency, was unrivaled in my experience with the medical profession.

"Please remove all your garments except your trousers, but empty your pockets. We need a true weight reading."

I snapped to and the nurse hustled me onto the scale. After measuring my weight, height and blood pressure, she read each result into a running tape recorder.

"You may dress now," she said and switched off the tape recorder. I could have sworn she goose-stepped out.

While I sweated back into my clothes and replaced my personal effects, Dr. Godwin asked a few routine questions about family diseases. Then, for the first time, he looked directly at me.

"Have you read my book?"

"Oh, yes. I think it's . . ."

"Good. You now know as much as I do about obesity and its statistically verified hazards to health and happiness. If you have any questions, reread it. It's all there."

I nodded, to convey that I understood the book with all its fragrant subtleties. I was puppy-eager for a returning nod or blink, any sign of approval. But Dr. Godwin's medium-sized hands were busy with three booklets he had plucked from three open-faced boxes on his desk. He half-extended them, causing me a moment of agonizing indecision: for me or not for me?

"These"—he fluttered the papers for emphasis—"are not to be found in my book. The results of ten years' work were not complete in time for publication. These booklets contain three diets. A, B, and C." He paused and looked at the pamphlets lovingly. "They will appear in the next edition so I'll explain them. Is that much clear, so far?"

I nodded, excitedly. On those pages I would find the formulas that would mean a new beginning.

"Now then," he resumed, "A is for the person who takes all of his meals at home and is marked 'Only for Home Eating.' B is for the person who takes all his meals away from home and is marked 'Only for Outside Eating.' C is for the person who travels part of the time for professional purposes and is marked 'Only for Professional Traveling Eating.' "

I enthused, "I take shows out of town often and . . ."

"These diets are the computerized results of ten years of my programmed feedings. They must be followed to the letter. They consist of three meals and three snacks every day, providing a vast amount of every kind of food to insure absolutely against any hunger. These diets have been tested on the obese, the normal and the undernourished with a ninety-eight percent success factor. The remaining two percent were medical abnormalities.

"These diets are so cross related that by following the simple A.C.C.—that stands for Asterisk Color Code —one may lose, gain or simply maintain weight. They also provide appropriate substitutions when circumstances unexpectedly change. If you're obliged to make a sudden trip, take an occasional meal at a strange place or simply have to take an isolated meal because of an emergency, you will find the appropriate contingency feeding by referring to the A.C.C. or Asterisk Color Code. By simply following the Asterisk Color Code, you have the built-in, computerized guarantee against any error."

He paused and almost smiled before continuing.

"There is a bonus. I said every variety of food. That includes candy, cake and, yes, ice cream. Well now, my nurse will arrange three appointments a week. You'll be billed bimonthly at the rate of fifteen dollars per consultation. That includes a vitamin complex of an original formula I've devised. Well, goodbye and good eating."

The nurse had silently filtered back sometime before Dr. Godwin finished. She handed him a syringe with one hand while assisting me off with my coat with the other. After the shot was administered, I was deftly turned over to a receptionist, who had the three booklets ready, plus four alternate schedules of appointments. I cleared my throat, which she took as choice number two, and presto! I found myself out in the wet street tilting at windmills, the New York version of flagging taxis in the rain.

After studying Dr. Godwin's diets, I acquired a new respect for those who prepare food. For one thing, their sophisticated language left me breathless: flake, scald, glaze, dredge, score, truss. This typical sampling of directions for food preparation invoked a usage of the English language completely foreign to me.

The "flake" I understood was like in corn, or dandruff. "Scald" was like in too hot a cup of coffee or abuse of some schnook. "Glaze" was like in punch drunk, once over lightly at rehearsal, streets in the winter after a freezing rain. "Dredge" was like in ruining local ecology, bringing up long-forgotten irrelevancies to win an argument, a political plum to a contractor who took three years to do it to a two-foot ditch. "Score" was like in . . . well, that one had gotten me into plenty of trouble all my life. I simply balked at "truss."

It all seemed hopeless until I thought of a brilliant solution: Why not give the charts to Vincent Sardi and let his chef handle it? Of course, this might bankrupt me in a few months, but by then, I'd be thin and swinging. For a moment, the fog lifted. But when I started with the Asterisk Color Code, I had trouble. Deep, deep trouble. Trouble with those "emergency and travel contingency feedings." Trouble with the instruction that if too busy to stop to eat, I should carry around "three sacks of alfalfa, sandwich wafers and two ounces of banana." The inviolable rule was never, but never, to be hungry, never to skip a meal or part of a meal or a snack or part of a snack, and every time I used the Asterisk Color Code, I had to record the occasion and color. No three reds, or two blues and a red, or a blue, red and yellow could recur within one seven-day period.

I developed an intermittent, high-frequency headache that lasted for three days. During a period of remission, I accepted the inevitable.

Dr. Godwin was not my bag.

now looked at my obesity in its broader aspects. That is to say, its social context. The vision of under-nourished children rose up to haunt me. And not just those in the United States. But all over the world, where millions were starving.

Somehow, just being a socially harmless fat man made me feel like a Nazi Party member in a Jewish neighborhood.

How could I even pretend I cared a damn about humanity when the food tonnage I inhaled could save the lives of many ravaged bodies? What further mon-strosities was I capable of if I could behave with such utter disregard for other human beings? Hadn't the world condemned the passive Nazi, even the non-Nazi, for criminally allowing genocide by his failure to op-pose it? And hadn't the excuse of ignorance of what was going on been mercilessly exposed as willful ignor-ance and, therefore, criminal?

How would any tribunal looking into the tragedy of starvation judge me? I didn't even have the excuse that my local Gauleiter ordered me to eat like a buffalo. No, I would stand damned to hell before any bar of justice as one who literally ate to the detriment of everybody, himself included. This indictment so shook me up that I solemnly took an oath to stop my cruel lack of concern with a huge segment of deprived human beings.

I began a systematic search for a doctor who would help me contribute to society. I quickly discovered that such a search was not unlike seeking a psychoanalyst, a lawyer, a surgeon or any other highly specialized professional. It was impossible to judge the ability of such a specialist except by the crudest means: his reputation and my intuition about him.

So I tried to educate myself a little by studying the most durable of the diet books. The Weight Watchers books by Jean Nidetch, Dr. Irwin Stillman's *Doctor's Quick Weight Loss Diet*, and *Stop Dieting, Start Losing* by Ruth West were but a few of the works I dug into.

I found one common denominator. All of the diets, if rigorously adhered to, had to work. All the suggestions, substitutions, tricks, games, techniques, in short, everything concerning how to lose weight and keep it off, were perfectly sound. Stripped of their individual preferences, they all bottom-lined out to one simple formula: cut the calories.

This conclusion was also shared by the not-so-famous diet books. In fact, excepting frauds and fads, the entire anti-obesity authorship was nothing more than a mixed bag of troubadours who sang one tune with endless variations. But if that's all there was to sing, why were new troubadours popping up every year?

In contrast to the silence that has existed these many years since the threat of smallpox has been eliminated, the market is glutted with resounding exhortations and methods to take excess fat off and keep it off. The conclusion was inescapable:

If all reducing diets could solve the problem, yet the problem remained unsolved, none could!!!

Well, I thought, so far, so lousy. Where do I go from here? Maybe a ninety-day hike on a large desert with only a long waterhose for a lifeline would do it.

All right, wise guy, I sternly rebuked myself, don't make the impossible take longer. Use your head for something other than an incinerator opening.

Zap! I got an idea. To be a dancer on Broadway, you had to be more than just crazy. You had to be in better shape than the greatest Commando of them all. The work was brutalizing. Yet of all people I have ever known, dancers never showed their age. I had been shocked many times to learn that this little girl was forty-five or that guy was pushing fifty. They were indestructible. And they knew the best specialists for every kind of disorder. They had to, in order to survive.

I got busy. After a dozen calls and repeated advice that I go to dancing class four hours every day to burn off the fat, one particular doctor was mentioned five times. A Swiss by the name of Manfred Zeitgeist. The dancers swore by him.

"He's marvelous, honest. I take a special shot and

eat whatever I want and never gain an ounce. I've been going to him for two years. And some of the kids have been seeing him for five years."

With smash notices from people whose livelihood depended upon much more than mere words, I was impressed enough to take a crack at this.

"Vell, my dear sir," Dr. Manfred Zeitgeist, a wizened, gray, gnomelike man began, "it's goot you know this theory from mine own tongue, mout and vords before starting zis treatment. You zee, zis formula of pregnant women's urrrine zimply brrreaks down fet vitout mercy and turns it to vawter vich collects in zee tissues. You will urrrinate kvite frekvently. Even in zee middle of a conversation, or often ven you are alzo eating. Zee remarkable zing iss you ectually urrrinate avay all zee excess shtuff. You vill come every day for my injectshuns. Oh yes, only vone detail. You must restrict your food intake to five hundred calories per day."

As I was trying to figure out a way to handle Dr. Zeitgeist's predictions of urinating while eating, his last words landed on me. I stopped the mental sandbox number. Five hundred calories per day would knock the weight off anyway. Why add urrrine to the prescription? I babbled some vaguery about checking my schedule and left.

That Swiss had a thing for urine, by God! I'd bet a month's micturition on it.

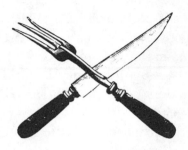

Two weeks had passed since the night I thought I'd eaten myself into a heart attack. I was still too afraid to tangle with the dangers of a complete meal, so I simply nibbled.

The word nibble suggested something graceful, dainty, a careless bite here and there between delicate pauses of conversation, or the absentminded reach for a morsel or two during a concentrated assault on some important piece of work.

I loosely defined all food that didn't require anything more than unwrapping before eating as a nibble. I'll just nibble, I decided, until I find the way out of my private caloric hell.

However, there was another important problem that needed clearing up immediately: my ill-advised and ill-timed marriage proposal to Carolyn. But the mere thought of revealing to her my "surprise" of fatter to slimmer on the way to the altar was too great an agony. That I had treated her so badly and called it love was unendurable. The more I thought of it, the less I could bear thinking of it. My only hope was to find Dr. Right-This-Way-to-Slenderhood before it was too late.

Exhausted from an entire day of postponing decisions, I clicked on the TV, seeking some diversion. But the major networks were on a kick of sickness and disease. Botulism in Hospital County, drug poisoning in Lawyertown and radioactive dandruff in Private Dickery.

I cranked over to another channel. David Susskind announced a panel discussion on obesity to be followed by a question period from the studio audience. Flanked by three eminent medical authorities, David began the discussion by asking the authorities whether the intake of water was important in weight loss.

Dr. X: "I recommend my patients drink ten glasses of water per day."

Dr. Y: "On the contrary, with most of my patients I restrict all intake radically, including water."

Dr. Z: "I don't regard the intake of water one way or another."

There was a flurry of water niggling, but David pounced on the obvious fact that the three eminent authorities really didn't differ all that much. They'd all agree, he was sure, it was a question of caloric intake. They did.

The doctors' discussion reached a dazzling height of illumination when David asked for questions. A lady blimp volunteered. She belonged to a group (or herd) whose members, after years of futile attempts to slim down, now accepted their bodies as they were, and stopped being unhappy over it. Would the doctors insist they trade their present state of happiness for their former misery?

To such an obviously loaded question, David unloaded a decisive question in reply: "Since happiness is a pursuit rather than a static state, isn't your pursuit hindered by your bulk as well as your significantly shortened life span in which to go on pursuing?"

The three eminent medical authorities waited for the applause to die and primly advised, "Obese people should never give up trying to lose weight."

"No matter what."

"Obesity is very unhealthy."

I clicked the goddamn set off and called my doctor.

"Frank? Herb."

"You feeling O.K.?"

"Fine. Listen, do you know a fat doctor I can see who can help me lose?"

"Fat doctor? What do you need a fat doctor for? Come into the hospital and I'll knock the weight off you like I did when you broke your legs."

"No, Frank. I can't live my life in hospitals. I've got to find another way."

"Maybe you're right. There's a no-nonsense man I know of with excellent credentials who specializes in treating obesity."

"Great. Who?"

"Dr. J. D. Elvis. He's listed in the book. Madison Avenue in the Sixties, I think. Let me know how it's going from time to time. And listen, just between you and me, Lenore . . ."

"Who?"

"My wife, Lenore. She needs to lose some weight. If this guy works for you, talk to her, will you? She won't listen to me."

Expecting to find human tonnage piled up ahead of me, I warily checked in at Dr. Elvis's premises fifteen minutes late. The waiting room didn't have one magazine out of place nor could one cigarette butt be found in the sparkling ashtrays, let alone a backlog of patients. In the act of sitting down, I saw a white-clad nurse enter smartly from the consulting area and ask:

"Mr. Greene?"

"Yes," I replied, reversing my impending flop into a chair. I felt an unpleasant twinge in my legs as my well-practiced sitting muscles had trouble untracking before giving way to my not-so-well-practiced standing muscles.

Dr. Elvis's nurse, in contrast to Dr. Godwin's white floater, had presence. She looked at her wristwatch quickly, but deliberately, as she said:

"This way, please."

Her delivery arrested my attention. I didn't have to be a musician to detect the subtle tone of reproof at my tardiness blending harmoniously with the implied expectation that the next time I would respect the rhythm of this medical establishment.

Dr. Elvis rose to greet me. Instantly, I was aware of a definitive, sharp, methodical person. His handshake was energetic, his eyes a clear gray-green and crinkled at the corners slightly as he smiled easily and waved me to sit. About fifty, his hair was full and attractively graying, his six-foot frame trim, without appearing fanatically athletic.

The office, a simple but elegant room, reflected the man. The bookshelves held volumes other than the usual depressing tomes of anatomy and pathology. I spotted some Shakespeare, Mark Twain, James Joyce and a few volumes of poetry. They looked frequently handled.

Without being obvious about it, he registered every move I made from the moment he laid eyes on me. His handshake, for instance, might have passed unnoticed, except that the circumstances alerted me and I sensed that he took note of the pressure I exerted, the length of time I clung to his hand and the manner in which I let go. He appeared to observe the way I lowered my bulk into the chair and how I arranged myself. And I was certain that he was quite alive to the attention I paid to his office library.

These split-second impressions took no more time in the aggregate than the action they accompanied. There was no awkward pause as we sat facing one another. Neither did he resort to that dreary ploy of fiddling with papers on his desk, since there weren't any, even for the sake of appearances. Nor were the inevitable silver-framed pictures of the wife and kids to be seen either. At precisely the instant a stall might have begun, he spoke.

"Mr. Greene, may we come to the point of your visit?" he asked pleasantly.

"Justice delayed is justice denied," I answered cheerily.

He laughed.

"That about sums it up." He paused. Not the pregnant pause, where the air is highly charged while the patient pays the freight. A short pause, with just time enough for a subtle shift of carriage, facial expression and a tiny adjustment of pitch, inflection and speed of speech for emphasis.

"There's little point in a thorough physical for you now. Pulse, respiration rate, cholesterol, blood sugar"—he flicked his hand as though brushing ants off a picnic basket—"are probably higher than a kite. I'd guess your blood pressure to be around two hundred diastolic."

"Should I sell when it hits two-ten?"

"You're holding a portfolio of volatile stocks, Mr. Greene, but those kind don't split. Their tendency is to bust wide open."

My hands got clammy. I felt a sudden nausea, or was this the beginning of the real thing? The old ticker about to quit? I couldn't even swallow. No spit.

Despite my well-known poker face that hid my very yellow streak, Dr. Elvis obviously knew he had me.

"In your case, it's better to postpone a complete workup until there's some semblance of order. Suppose we set a target date of D minus forty: diet less forty pounds. Then we'll know if any damage you've done is permanent. Here's a simple diet you don't even have to write down, let alone be a gourmet cook. Breakfast: half a grapefruit, water, black coffee or tea. Dry. That means no sugar. Lunch: the same, plus one sliced tomato without salt. Dinner: three ounces of broiled fish, fowl or lean meat and a small lettuce and tomato salad without oil or salt. Get a food scale so you don't guess. Between meals, water, coffee or tea. Same thing after meals. And of course, no alcohol. Any questions?"

"Can I have some seltzer?" I asked meekly.

"Yes. All you want."

I sighed gratefully. "Well, that's some . . ."

"For bathing. If you're partial to bubble bath."

I flushed, fury and respect playing tug of war inside me. He went on.

"This diet is simple and effective. It will burn off anywhere from five to ten pounds a week. If you're not absolutely rigid about it, then there's no point in your consulting me because I have no magic, no quick remedies up my sleeve."

He paused again, as though waiting to see how my tug of war turned out. I was also awaiting its outcome. Would I tell him to screw a concrete wall or salute and say, "Yes, sir"?

"One more thing, Mr. Greene. I see patients only once a week. For medical reasons, not for hand holding. More than that is not only unnecessary, but unspeakably unethical. A medical diploma is no license to practice extortion."

The tug of war came to an abrupt finish. I went limp, flooded with gratitude that Dr. Elvis didn't try snowing me with a bunch of shots, shine and shinola.

I broke into a grin.

"Well, that's about it. Before you go, let's have a look at your weight and blood pressure. Just for the record."

After the scale thing, which I couldn't see without my reading glasses, he pumped up the cold silk noose around my arm and watched the gauge as the air hissed out.

"Hmm," he intoned almost whimsically, "I advise you to sell, Mr. Greene. At two-twenty over one-ten, you're pressing your luck."

I lost eleven and one-half pounds the first week. A week that was full of surprises. Instead of a bleak, depressed succession of tormenting hours stretching out beyond the horizon, I was positively euphoric. Each hunger pang, every unpleasant stomach gurgle, any painful tug and pull for food only enhanced my euphoria. In fact, I positively looked for symptoms of discomfort. The greater the ache, the deeper the twinge, the sharper the gnaw, the better I felt.

But this wasn't the well-known religious ecstasy of redemption through suffering, the light-headedness of fasting. Nor the wages of sin falling due in the payoff of masochism. Far simpler, each nasty stitch was an indisputable piece of evidence that I was not only capable of an impressive degree of self-mastery, but that I could endure its grim moments with what amounted to contempt. For a man whose will had been imprisoned by the tyranny of his appetite, every stab of hunger was nothing less than a mighty leap forward to freedom. Freedom from unwanted want.

Living by myself with this liberation for just one week was all I could handle. I had to open a valve to share, not simply let off, some of the steam I was generating. It was time to put a stop to those fitful telephone starts with Carolyn.

"Carolyn? Behold, I am the new wave resurrection," I exulted.

"Herb? Is that you again?" She sounded funny.

"Did I wake you? Is it too early again?" I asked with great presence of mind at three in the afternoon. "Listen, about last week, you never answered me. Will you?"

"Will I what?"

"You know, marry me." I felt sure that by repeating my romantic proposal, she'd be reassured about everything.

"Why sure, I'll marry you. I'll get a few telephone operators as bridesmaids, you can get a justice of the peace on a conference call and we'll phone in the ceremony. After all, you've been phoning in the courtship."

"You're upset."

"Me upset? Why should I be upset? You ask me to marry you, you don't wait for my answer and you hang up on me. I call you back and you hang up on me again. I call you for days and days and I'm told you're out of town. So why should I be upset over a little thing like that?"

"Well, one of the reasons I called, as a matter of fact, was to apologize."

"All right then. Get to it."

"I apologize."

I waited anxiously.

"You're crazy," she said, but some of the sharpness had gone from her voice.

"You've got to admit anything this nutty must be legitimate. Nobody's smart enough to make it up. Besides, I love you—how long before your tour is over?"

"I love you, and I finish the tour in six weeks. Let's get married then."

I calculated quickly: Eleven and a half pounds a week, twenty-three pounds in two weeks, could be forty-six pounds in four weeks plus fourteen pounds more in maybe ten days minus plateaus where I'd retain water and give or take a week or so for metabolic irregularities . . . I figured six weeks. But I played it safe.

"No, in about six and three-quarter weeks."

"Six and three-quarter weeks. Hmm. That sounds like a nice, round figure, all right." She paused briefly. "Honey? Why the three-quarters?"

"That's when I . . . well, that's when this whole project will be finished."

"What is the project?"

"Well now, that's the point. It's kind of a surprise wedding present."

"Can't you give me a hint?"

"I'm doing this essentially for you, but it'll be great for both of us."

"Is it . . ."

"No fair. It's a surprise. No more hints. O.K.?"

"All right. When will I see you?"

I calculated quickly again. "Weekend after next."

With any luck that would be twenty-three pounds later. A grand total of thirty-four and a half pounds.

"Can't you make it next weekend?"

"No, oh no. I'll be smack in the middle of the worst of it. I need fourteen days at the very least."

"Well, O.K.," she said regretfully. "Two weeks then. And don't work too hard. I miss you."

"I miss you too." And I did. Very much. So much so, that it only strengthened my resolve to stay away from her until there was no danger she'd be repelled by me.

I made it to Dr. Elvis's office right on the nose of my appointment. I hoped he'd be a little late. For two reasons. First, I wanted to replay my conversation with Carolyn and enjoy being engaged for 6¾ weeks. Secondly, I planned a routine of watch-looking and appointment-announcing to get even with both him and his nurse for their smart-ass little reproofs on my first visit.

But they headed me off at the pass. Madame Penicillin cracked the inner door just as I closed the outer one. Leaning through the opening, she smiled professionally and said, "Good afternoon, Mr. Greene. Just come right in." Pushing the door wide open, she waited for me to walk the twenty feet across the reception room. Three steps before I crossed the threshold, she shot a look at her wristwatch with the barest wisp of prim satisfaction. My respect for her was firmly established. This was nursemanship of a high order.

Dr. Elvis barely restrained a knowing smile as I briskly entered his office, in sharp contrast with the shuffle I had managed the week before. Instead of sitting down, I asked eagerly, "Should I get on the scale?" I was bursting to see his reaction.

"In a little while. You know the number and I can pretty much guess at it."

Anxious to please and surprise him, and dying to show off, I smiled.

"You said this diet would burn off between five to ten pounds a week. How much would you guess I dropped, Doctor?"

"I'd estimate your loss at between eleven and one-half and eleven and three-quarter pounds," he answered without a moment's hesitation.

That took the wind out of my sails and I dropped into a chair. But in no time, I made another attempt to win his approval. I wanted him to know how much faith I had in him.

"But doesn't that raise the average?"

"No. I've had patients drop fifteen, twenty and twenty-five pounds the first week. In fact, your drop is statistically on the medium-low side. The average first-week weight loss is exactly sixteen-point-two pounds. The record holder in my files broke thirty-five pounds. Of course, he was somewhat larger than you. He weighed in at three hundred fifty pounds, stripped and dry."

I could tell by now that this was no pat-on-the-back, sloshy operation that Dr. Elvis ran. He pulled no punches, glossed over no facts and indulged in no elaborate optimism. This led me to admit that my enthusiasm was premature and my need to win his praise quite childish. Well, I certainly wanted him to know that I got his message, that I could meet him on objective ground. In fact, I was particularly eager that he know I understood.

"Aren't you saying, Dr. Elvis, that jumping is fine exercise, but if it's to conclusions, it's not fine or even exercise?"

"Not quite. I was merely informing you of the facts as far as I know them."

"Oh," I breathed. Then to my acute embarrassment, I realized that I was asking for approval again. I decided to drop all further attempts to get a pat on the head and to level with him instead.

"I just said 'oh' as if I knew what you were driving at. But if you'd asked, 'Oh, what?' I would have had to say 'Oh, I don't know.' The truth is, I was disappointed at your reaction to my losing eleven and a half pounds."

Dr. Elvis flicked a finger as though none of this was worth more than that tiny gesture to brush it away.

"My reaction is irrelevant, Mr. Greene. What does it have to do with your losing weight in any case?"

I thought that one over before answering.

"Nothing, really. I suppose the whole thing boils down to next week's results and the next and so on. Obviously, if I came here for your help, then I can assume you'll try to help and wish for our mutual success."

Dr. Elvis shook his head.

"I can't help you, Mr. Greene. I can only advise you of the measures you must take to help yourself. And I must look after your medical needs. As for wishing, I'm afraid that's best left in the hands of fairy tale writers."

"Yeah," I agreed glumly. "That, I guess, settles that."

"An inspired guess, Mr. Greene. Well, for my records, would you get on the scale, please?"

I had a funny notion that I had just dropped another pound in pure sweat. Dr. Elvis adjusted the weights and counterweights meticulously and announced:

"You lost exactly eleven pounds and seven ounces this past week. Just one ounce short of eleven and one-half pounds."

This announcement shredded what little poise I had left. The extra ounce felt like a fifty-pound lead weight.

"Goddammit!" I exploded at the scale.

Dr. Elvis laughed.

I buttoned up my coat all thumbs and left the office looking as though I was wearing a very crooked straitjacket.

By the time I got home, the depression caused by my stupid rage lifted and was replaced by a mysterious feeling of expectation. The certainty that something was imminent became so strong that I plopped into my easy chair to wait. While the intensity of my feeling didn't diminish, its nature changed by tiny degrees. Only after the change was complete did I realize that the mysterious expectation had been nothing more than a tugging need to fill the vacuum created by the loss of my euphoria. The instant I recognized this, I felt I was being sucked into and drowned in waves of time.

The next two weeks stretched out before me like

some vast sea. I could see each wave boil up in the distance and rise monstrously as it approached. I could delay the tide, but not prevent it. And for every moment's delay I imposed, the pressure and size would swell even more obscenely before I would give way to its crash and crush. The torrent swamped me, smashed the breath out of me, anesthetized my senses and finally paralyzed my will to fight for my life.

I leaped out of my chair as though the vision was a reality and began pacing my room. I soon discovered why prisoners paced. My pacing absorbed and released every last current of tension, focusing my attention on the bend of my knee, the rise and fall of my feet. The monotonous rhythm and sound of my footsteps captured and held my mind hypnotically.

But the most remarkable thing was that once started, pacing required no effort to continue. It was utterly self-sustaining. Even when I became aware of its doom-laden similarity to my waking nightmare, it nevertheless took considerable effort to stop.

Although it was only early evening, I'd had enough of this day. I took a whooping dose of sleeping pills and sank into drugged oblivion.

During the next couple of days, I called Carolyn every three hours or so.

I arranged with Lucia Prego, the capable public relations woman at the Ambassador East in Chicago, to have a dozen roses sent up to Carolyn's room every hour on the hour. On each accompanying card was one word. Only when the last card arrived, and all were arranged alphabetically, would an intelligible message emerge. I spent most of the time happily working out this crazy cipher:

ABSTEMIOUS BACHELOR CLAIMS DESPERATION ECLIPS-
ING FELICITIOUS GLANDULAR HEDONISM, INTERDICTED
JOCUNDITY . . .

I got hung up for awhile on the letter K.

Between the calls and boiling in my alphabet soup, I sandwiched in a couple of errands. The first one was to my tailor. I brought him three favorite outfits I planned to take on my visit to Carolyn. One was much too small, one almost made it and the last was much too large. I requested alterations that would fit exactly right, ten days later, when I would be eighteen pounds lighter.

Giovanni, a master craftsman from the Old World, was doubtful.

"Eighteen pounds less, Mr. Greene? Omma don't know where you gonna lose 'em."

"All over, Giovanni. Take a couple of pounds from the back, some more from the front, and the rest of the places you have to take in, and add them up to eighteen pounds. Then do the opposite on the suit you have to let out."

Giovanni was no longer doubtful.

"Omma tella you, Mr. Greene. Why you no buy new suits ten days later? Itsa no trouble then."

"Because in about two and three-quarter weeks after that, Giovanni, I'll be another twenty-five pounds less."

Giovanni's black eyes dimmed in confusion. I tried a different tack.

"Look, Giovanni, this is important. A very special occasion. Amore. You know. Love."

The poor man began showing signs of depression. This puzzled me. It was inconceivable that his Italian temperament didn't fire him up to an enthusiastic and instant solution.

"What measurementsa you gonna want?"

"Measurements? Well, let's see." I put one hand on my back, one on my middle and pushed madly to what I thought my waist would be after losing eighteen pounds. "Measure me now, Giovanni," I gasped, "this'll be about right."

"Your chest, Mr. Greene, she'sa look pretty damn big when you push in your stomach lika that."

I let go and collapsed, coughing. I pleaded with him.

"Giovanni, I've been a customer here for years. You have a long file on me. Look, you made these three suits yourself. You know what I look like fat, skinny or in the middle. I know you can do it. Anyway, it doesn't have to be a perfect fit."

My last remark was a mistake. Giovanni was stricken.

"Not fit? Not fitta perfect? Mr. Greene, have you ever walked outa Giovanni's shop with clothes not fitta perfect? Mama mia, thisa cut me like a knife in the heart. People woulda say Giovanni no gooda tailor. People woulda say Giovanni no more honesta man."

In the end, we compromised. He agreed to alter the large suit on the condition that I come for fittings every two days. The small suit was rejected. The one close to a reasonable fit was no longer fashionable, so it was discarded. And just to insure his reputation and pride in craftsmanship, nothing less than a brand-new suit would do. He would mold that during the frequent fittings. As I was leaving, Giovanni stipulated one further condition.

"Mr. Greene, I maka this only causa you a long-time customer and nice gentleman. But I can't change in the middle. You say you lose eighteen pounds, you gotta sticka to eighteen pounds. Otherwise, the clothing, she'sa no gonna fit."

My next trip was to Cartier's, that graceful establishment of taste and elegance. The window display arrested my attention and stimulated my ambition to make money. Jewelry of modest price discreetly blended with $20,000 rubies. Handwrought clips and brooches were casual neighbors of their less opulent cousins. I tore myself away and went in.

I was approached by a distinguished-looking man, whose carriage, dress and beautifully styled graying hair suggested a United Nations diplomat moonlighting on his day off.

"Can I be of help, sir?"

Whether I imagined a more than usual inspection or not testified to the man's subtlety as well as to my somewhat disreputable appearance. My clothes were chosen with one purpose in mind: comfort, or what came closest to that. So the tweed sport jacket that I wore open because it wouldn't quite button didn't really match the baggy, jet black mohair trousers, and these were plaited at the waist by a tight belt. Sweating through Giovanni's edition of Dante's Inferno had done nothing for my hair either.

"You certainly can be of help, but I'm hoping that you also may be of help," I flashed some grammar at him.

"I hope so, too," the man answered.

"May I see some teardrop earrings?" I asked, and unnecessarily added, "diamonds."

He deadpanned: "Certainly, sir. Diamonds. If you'll step this way."

His delivery was so good, he might just as well have said: "Cartier's does not share merchandise with

Woolworth's. Only an occasional customer, and that is unavoidable because of the law."

He showed me a couple of blinding sparklers. I played with them for a minute.

"How much are they?"

"Twenty-five thousand dollars."

"I see."

"Plus tax, of course."

I got his continuing message, the louse. Oh, how I wished for a heavy bank account! That would cause my seediness to blossom to quaintness.

"Would you care to see something less formal? Perhaps more spare, more petit?"

"Indeed."

Out came another pair of gems, less formal, or as he meant it, less expensive, but still quite beautiful. Sixteen hundred plus tax. Out of nowhere, I got the feeling that the "spare" and "petit" thing was aimed at my not-so-spare nor petit belly.

"Very nice. I'll write you a check, but I'd rather not take the earrings just now. Would you send them on with a messenger later in the morning?"

That little ploy was to let him know he could check my bank account until his eyes fell out.

"Certainly, sir." His manner began to shift. He added the tax to the sixteen hundred and handed it to me.

He'd fallen into the trap.

"Oh, no, not those. The more formal style."

That nailed him. He scribbled a little and handed me the new total. I took out my checkbook and casually wrote the check. But at precisely the instant he reached for it, I gently withdrew my hand and mused.

"You may be right after all. These are too formal. I'll take the others."

Making a big display of tearing up the check, I wrote another one. I gave him my address and phone number and congratulated myself on leaving a seasoned Cartier's man more than a bit shook.

The instant I hit the street, I felt sick. Why had I done such a cruel thing to a guy just doing his job? And why the hell was I so sure he was shafting me? And if he was, why had I provoked it? Why?

The answer was as simple as it was nauseating: I was fat and he was not. I had felt naked, on parade and humiliated. I needed a patsy to diffuse the unendurable shame and insufferable embarrassment of being fat. From now on, my diet would have to include some humble pie.

As the time for my departure approached, my confidence grew. So did the dividends of A.T.&T. from my long-distance calls. As did Giovanni's inventory of pins that my frequent fittings required.

The diet had become routine. I had stocked up on grapefruit, lettuce and tomatoes, a five-pound white-meat turkey roll, ditto chicken roll and a few pounds of broiled filet of sole that was stacked in three-ounce, air-tight packages in the refrigerator. So once a day I sliced three ounces of turkey or chicken or simply grabbed a packet of the sole along with a tomato and a couple of leaves of lettuce. I rotated the entree every day. This was simple, neat, entailed no cooking or menu making, very infrequent trips to the market to buy fresh lettuce and tomatoes and hardly any dish-washing at all. Not only did it simplify housekeeping, but was gratifyingly easy on the budget. Dieting wasn't all drag and no fun, I noted happily.

I even found that my scant dinners were sometimes superfluous. On Thursday, two days before I was to see Carolyn, I simply forgot to eat. This astonished me. I had skipped meals on other diets, of course, but only through clenched teeth and a steely resolve not to give in to my whim of iron. But spontaneous food amnesia was a whole new business. A business that I assumed to be monopolized by the blessed slender. I'd have traded my interest in heaven for a piece of the action, and here it was, free, on a beautiful, glorious, deliciously empty platter.

As I waded through my Friday schedule, I marveled at the subtlety of Dr. Elvis. It simply couldn't be sheer coincidence that I'd busted into a hitherto mysterious and impregnable fortress. That man had to have a bit of magic up his sleeve. I supposed that when the time came, he'd either tell me what it was or I would see it for myself.

I was impatient for my appointment to see how the forgotten meal would show up on his scale. Punctually at 4:00 P.M., I sailed into his office.

"What's up, Doc? Lay you heavy odds it's not my weight."

He smiled. "In your circumstances, long odds would be a more fortunate description than heavy odds."

"Touché," I said with a grin. "Oh, by the way, I'm flying to Chicago for the weekend."

"Work or play?" he asked matter-of-factly.

"Play. But the serious kind."

He nodded but made no comment.

"But don't worry, really. You see, I plan to take my food scale along, just to be on the safe side," I assured him.

"I know of no reason to worry, Mr. Greene. But perhaps you do."

I shook my head, a little put out. The man never gave an inch. I got a flash. Maybe that was part of his secret weapon. I dismissed my flash in another flash. I really didn't give a damn at the moment. I wanted to get on that scale.

"Well, shall we get to it?" I asked, jerking my head in its direction.

"Certainly."

I got on and he did his number with the weights. It seemed to me that he took longer than usual. Then, apparently satisfied, he walked away and sat down before announcing the result. I resumed my seat somewhat excited. I was getting to know Dr. Elvis and was pretty sure he was deliberately stalling in order to dramatize the result. Perhaps as a weekend send-off.

"You've gained one pound, Mr. Greene."

I began to laugh.

"That was the greatest one-line delivery I ever heard," I said. "You should have been in show business."

"You should have been on your diet."

There was something in his tone that stopped my next laugh halfway down my throat. I shook my head.

"That's impossible."

"Nothing's impossible, Mr. Greene. Even staying on your diet."

I boiled over.

"Either you're trying to gaslight me, Doctor, or your goddamn scale has gone fruit. I broke that lousy diet yesterday. But not by eating. By forgetting to eat."

Dr. Elvis didn't bat an eye at my outburst, nor did he disbelieve me.

"Well, then, without benefit of hysteria, we'll have to look elsewhere for the answer. What did you have yesterday and today in the way of water, tea or coffee?"

"Let's see now. I've been running around getting organized for my weekend in Chicago, so I drop in for black coffee between errands. And I knock off a few cups during long phone conversations. I've probably consumed a couple of gallons these past two days."

"There's your answer. You haven't expelled all that water yet. But you probably will get rid of most of it within twenty-four to forty-eight hours. However, may I caution you not to observe your former food habits in your consumption of liquids. There are better uses for the human head than to emulate a pig at a trough."

I was so relieved that Dr. Elvis uncovered the reason for my weight that I barely noticed the cutting comparison. Besides, it was all too true and a more delicate phrase would not have changed the facts.

I zipped home. For the next few hours my activity was rather confined and narrow. From time to time I detected a faint echo of that obsessed Swiss, Dr. Zeitgeist, rolling his guttural R's as he reveled through the "delights of urrrinating."

At about 9 P.M., the high tide receded. As Carolyn was in the theater, I settled down to wait out the couple of hours until I could phone her. Then I felt a bit hungry and remembered I had forgotten to eat again. Two days successively, I gloated. Well, I thought, I was entitled, at the very least, to Thursday's dinner. But I was in no hurry. I kind of hemmed and hawed and stalled until I decided I might as well get it over with. I didn't want to risk feeling heady or dizzy for tomorrow's flight.

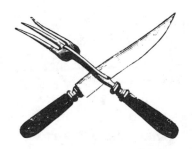

I was awakened by an assortment of my own snorts and audible yawns. My eyes fluttered open in the muted light of a shade-drawn room. I stretched and knocked the telephone off the night table. Sitting up, I rubbed my eyes and bent over to pick it up. It was whining a continuous note, disagreeably high in pitch. I got out of bed, replaced the receiver in its cradle and stared at it. Something didn't seem quite right.

After a bit, I realized I had only knocked the receiver down. The cradle at the far end of the table was well out of stretch range. Slowly, I gathered that the phone must have been off the hook. A dense foreboding enveloped me.

I sat down on the edge of the bed, trying to collect myself, but a sizable part of me was resisting that very thing. The two opposing forces were so evenly matched there was a momentary calm, and it seemed to me I was the battleground rather than the combatants. The sensation, though sinister and threatening, was almost enjoyable, like a familiar danger.

All at once the battle broke out and I was bombarded by a shower of red-hot memories:

". . . entitled, at the very least, to Thursday's dinner."

"Why not in addition to Friday's?"

The knife poised over the turkey loaf, wavering, but not slicing Thursday's or Friday's ration.

The internal argument raging: "Friday's dinner does not include Thursday's missed dinner."

"What possible harm could it do since it will have become a part of the correct daily intake when averaged over a week?"

"But Thursday is past, and to treat Friday as the sum of Thursday and Friday is ridiculous. Thursday's three ounces plus Friday's three ounces equals six ounces in one day!"

"Equal equals equal."

The knife cut any further argument as it carved Thursday and Friday into one heap.

The last swallowed morsel turned sour. What had I done? With a couple of bites, with a few measly mouthfuls, I had destroyed everything. Three ounces had ruined my hopes, had proven once and for all that I could never find the strength to stick to it.

A tiny, drowning rational part of me made one valiant attempt: "But three ounces equals three ounces, not total ruin, not hopelessness, only three ounces."

With self-contempt, I repeated: "Only three ounces, only three ounces, they might as well be three tons."

And with those three terrible ounces, my drowning

rational self went under for the third time and disappeared.

And so did the turkey roll. And the chicken roll. And the filet of sole. And a host of hastily gathered additions that were delivered between naps, all through Friday night, past the plane departure on Saturday, past its arrival in Chicago.

I heaved myself off the bed in order to stop the terrible memory-picture parade. But once on my feet, I merely stood woodenly in place. Then, as if it mattered, I wondered what time it was. I peered through the dimness at the illuminated clock dial: two o'clock.

Two o'clock.

Two o'clock. Two o'clock. Two o'clock.

It had a good hypnotic rhythm. Excellent for obliterating unwanted thoughts. The old, orthodox jazz beat that the drummer initiated and kept going throughout certain up-tunes.

Two o'clock. Two o'clock. Two o'clock. Piano and bass in now. Two o'clock. Two o'clock. Two o'clock.

The front-door buzzer cut off the din. I stumbled out of the bedroom and almost opened the door before realizing I was stark naked.

"Who's there?" I asked.

"Herb? It's me, Natalie."

"Who??"

"Natalie. Natalie Wood."

I had to get into some clothes quickly.

"Just a minute, Natalie. Just a minute."

I switched on the living-room light and saw sickening remains of food on three or four plates. I gathered a couple up and plunged into the kitchen. The sink was full and the counter space littered with paper sacks. I quickly stacked them in the refrigerator, trying to invent reasons for the mess. It seemed very important.

Then I headed for the bathroom door where my robe hung. I struggled into it, cracked an elbow against a sharp edge and shuffled to the door, frantically trying to use my fingers as a comb to get the tangles out of my hair. My two-day stubble felt like quills.

I had my hand on the knob when I realized the whole apartment must smell of stale food. I dashed to the window, raised the shade and opened it wide. A bare wisp of air came in.

I unlatched the door. Natalie and a tall young man filed in.

"You'll have to excuse this, Natalie," I said with a sweep of my arm, "but I had a little party here last night and today being Sunday, the maid is off. And I..."

"I'm the one who should do the apologizing. I tried calling you for hours and hours, but after all the busy signals, I had the phone company check and they said your telephone was off the hook."

I nodded. "Yeah, probably some drunk. I just saw it and put it back. Uh . . . sit down. Can I get you some coffee?"

"No thanks," she said. "We can only stay a minute. I'm rushing to catch a plane back to L.A. I just wanted you to meet Andrew Whaling, my hairdresser. He writes divine lyrics. Please look at his work and give him your opinion. I think he's great."

I shook hands with Andrew Whaling. He took out a sheaf of typewritten pages and handed them to me.

Natalie said tactfully, "You don't have to do it now. I just wanted you to know that I recommend Andrew, that's all. Well, we'd better go or I'm going to miss my plane."

After they left, I dropped the papers on the piano, and sat heavily on the bench. Then I saw a sight that must have made my party story to Natalie appear ridiculous.

Arranged across the couch, and leaving no room for seating, was my brand-new Mark Cross traveling bag partially packed with socks, underwear, handkerchiefs and shirts. Beside the bag were two pairs of new shoes and an open jewelry box that displayed Carolyn's earrings. Next in line was my brand-new Mark Cross leather shaving kit, wide open for packing, and last was my plane ticket in its virgin American Airlines envelope.

Party? Well, why didn't I have the presence of mind to say going-away party?

Then I noticed the four new books I bought were scattered on the floor, a couple bearing smeary grease stains. A third had a slice of salami stuck in the middle, apparently serving as a bookmark.

The room had turned cold. I got up to shut the window but stared out at the sky instead. The overcast resembled a blanket of oozing gruel that gradually congealed as it absorbed the rising benefits of modern city life.

I knew I would miss Carolyn as long as I lived. I was quite certain that the latest "Mr. Greene-is-out-of-town" bleat from my answering service had killed what little chance there was of a life with her. But I couldn't bear thinking about my cowardice in removing the phone from its hook so as not to hear its ring.

I shut the window, flopped into a chair, and shifted around to relieve a nagging itch in the small of my back. The mild relief was the first uncomplicated pleasure I had experienced in some forty hours. The recognition that I was still capable of experiencing some pleasure, superficial and fleeting as this one was, was surprising. Contemplating it, I realized that having lost everything, I no longer expected anything. I imagined I must be reaching a unique state of calm, bearing no relation to serenity. Now that I knew the worst, I felt unburdened. At least I was free of the unbearable pressure of a hopeless fight.

I thought about Skinny. And felt no overwhelming nostalgia for his amusing, if not always agreeable, visits. But, I supposed, I would miss him now and again. He was challenging in his tart way and therefore diverting. My way of life would no longer require nor benefit from his services. Of that I was beyond doubt. And with my doubts about my way of life gone, Skinny would have nothing to bite on, nothing to grab. No conflicts to expose, no contradictions to show, no split feelings he could play upon—in short, no resistance to overcome. And without meeting my resistance, there was no way for him to build up any pressure. It would simply dissipate the instant he tried to apply it. Well, as he himself admitted, I had invented him. Now I would simply put him to rest. But he was wrong about one thing: I didn't really dislike him, no matter what I said in a moment of pique.

It began to rain, a steady soft rain. Soon the windowpanes were so densely studded with droplets that it was difficult to see. I squinted and squeezed my eyes tightly together in the thoughtless notion that by clearing them, I could see through the window.

Instead of sharper vision, the window dissolved in a greater blur. I wondered how long I had been silently weeping.

I was puzzled at the phenomenon that while my eyes were overflowing, the rest of me remained unaffected.

Neither the warmth of my tears, their salty taste nor their heavy spill brought forth an answering sob or even a heartfelt pang. I made no effort to dam the flow or to resist any feeling. But I was getting wet, so I reached for a bunched-up old Kleenex in the pocket of my robe, dabbed at my face and eyes and blew my nose. And detected the lingering odor of food on the tissue. This was unseemly at the moment, so I got up, fetched a fresh box of tissues and returned to my chair.

Presently, my eyes simply stopped tearing. I splashed cold water on my face and waited for some reaction I could define or at least label. I felt sad rather than tragic, dislocated but not lost, empty yet not hollow and, finally, drained rather than numb.

I wandered back to the bedroom and bleakly considered going out to see a movie, just to get away from myself for awhile. As I pulled off my robe and got into a pair of shorts, I noticed the telephone and near it the clock. Six o'clock and the thing hadn't rung once. Well, that meant that Carolyn had finally seen through all my stupid deceptions and pictured me in the full-blown glory of my bloat. She must be feeling tremendous relief at having escaped in the nick of time.

I returned to the living room to get some socks out of the sprawling suitcase. Then I decided to check whether the rain had let up. It was too dark to see anything outdoors. But before approaching the window clad only in jockey shorts and risking a peek from some stray voyeur in a neighboring building, I clicked off the lights.

As I walked across my darkened living room, I felt a surge of relief that the picture I presented was blacked out. Jockey shorts stretched to their absolute limit of elasticity and overhung by a flabby mass that bounced and jiggled with every step I took. I cursed the goddamn apartment-dwelling life style for obliging me to stay alert against the lurid possibilities of window watchers.

What the hell was this society coming to? If you didn't get robbed, mugged, raped or murdered, you had to take ridiculous measures to forestall the thousand prying eyes of your friendly neighborhood degenerates.

I had been staring out the window during the latter part of this unspoken tirade but could see nothing through my rage. So I concentrated on the meteorological conditions. It was still raining steadily enough, although with a change. A misty spray was floating down on cushions of air. Apparently, somebody up there got impatient with pelting the stuff and simply hung a superfine screen under the cloud deck, leaving it to drip dry.

I backed away from the window wondering whether the stylish raincoat I'd bought after my accident would cover enough of me to keep me from getting soaked. I sat down to consider the possibilities but a familiar voice interrupted.

"Fatso? It's me. Skinny. I owe you an apology."

"Apology?" I asked incredulously. "Apology for what?"

"For Dr. Elvis."

"Dr. Elvis? I don't get it. Why?"

"Because Dr. Elvis is a first-rate, solid, through and through bastard."

"How do you figure that?"

"The son of a bitch had you on a put-down diet. And it's all my fault, Fatso. All my fault. I'm very sorry."

I took some time to digest this.

"I'll admit that Dr. Elvis was rough, but . . ."

"Rough? He came on like a barracuda!"

"Well, he said right off that he wasn't going to hold my hand."

"That's it. The setup. He could always nail you no matter what, because the subject was fat. So you lose. Did he ever meet you on neutral ground?"

"But I didn't go to him for neutral ground. I'm fat and went to him for help."

"But you're a human being, and he's supposed to be one too. So where was the help in getting yourself brained?"

"Yeah. Why would he do a thing like that?"

"Look, Elvis is one of the growing crop of doctors who don't even remember what to prescribe for a stuffy nose. So, in order to look and feel important, they go into the 'fat' business, where they can never be wrong. All they have to do is to say, 'You are fat, you should eat less.' And there's very big money in it for them."

"You have a point there."

"Point, hell! That's the whole ballgame."

"But what's that got to do with you?"

"Well, I put the screws to you as though you were a piece of wood. I kept needling, insulting, pushing you, leaning on you without letup, without one shred of sympathy. So, it was only natural, after that much brainwashing, you'd find someone else who'd do the same thing and take money for it too."

I saw the point.

"Why couldn't I be an alcoholic instead? At least I'd have the excuse of not knowing what I'm doing."

"I owe you an apology for that one also."

"Apology again? Why?"

"I let you think alcoholism and drug addiction are tougher to handle than obesity. But that's not quite true. Think of it: Suppose an alcoholic had to have three drinks or an addict three fixes a day to keep from starving to death. Treatment would be hopeless. But that's exactly what you have to do. Just to stay alive, you must have food, the very thing that's like booze to a drunk or dope to a junkie."

"Now what do I do?"

"For one thing, don't let me or anyone else ever again beat you with a baseball bat and pretend it's good exercise for you. And don't beat yourself, for God's sake. Ease up. Turn off the torture switch. Don't make any final judgments."

"Sure, sure. But what do I do for an encore after these last couple of days?" I asked bitterly.

The door buzzer sounded.

Skinny snorted. "If that's Elvis, kick him in the head. I'll be seeing you."

I stumbled in the dark to find the light switch. Completely forgetting I was in my shorts, I opened the door.

Carolyn, after waiting for me to say something, crisply announced, "I want to talk to you, Herb. May I come in?"

She took the shocked bobbing of my head for an answer and brushed past me. I simply touched the door, which flew shut, and flexed my toes, which propelled me into the room. I stopped short of banging into her by going limp and vibrating madly in place.

She took in the sights before turning around.

I struggled to work up just a little spit to unstick my tongue from the roof of my mouth. It didn't happen.

"I think you owe me some kind of an explanation. Without hiding behind an answering-service operator," she said. Her face was set and determined, but she couldn't quite control a tremble in her lower lip.

My mouth remained a dry, hardened glue pot. She waited until there was no waiting left in her. Her shoulders slackened and her voice changed from its pent-up challenging staccato to a cool reserve.

"Well, that's that. I'm sorry I broke in on you."

She started out. At the sight of her movement, words ripped out of my guts and burned past my throat.

"Don't go, Carolyn. I love you. That hasn't changed. Don't go. Please don't go."

She stopped, looked deeply into my face and put down her overnight case. She searched my eyes for another moment before she spoke.

"I could use a drink."

I had shot my bolt with the few words and could do no more than to remain silently rooted in place. She guided me to my chair, helped me sit and asked:

"Where do you keep it?"

I didn't trust myself to utter a sound, so I used sign language. She got the general idea and headed for the small liquor cabinet. She poured a stiff shot and took a good swallow.

She remained standing, her gaily colored plastic raincoat reflecting the light from the ceiling fixture. My voice returned.

"What about Chicago? I mean the show?" I stupidly asked.

"Today is Sunday. I'm not due on stage until eight forty-five tomorrow night. So, I've got a little better than twenty-four hours."

"That's right," I said idiotically. I made a feeble attempt to get to my feet, but the effort was ruinous.

"I think you should sit down, at least," I wheezed while trying the impossible.

She finished her drink, took off her coat and draped

it over her overnight case. Then she threaded her way through the book-strewn floor to the sofa, the cluttered sofa with the half-finished bits and pieces of my aborted travel plan. She closed my suitcase, put it on the floor and sat down.

After a moment, she asked quietly, "Is there another woman?"

"Another? . . . No. No other woman. Only you."

"Then are you an alcoholic?"

I shook my head.

"No, I'm not an alcoholic. But I might as well be one."

"You mean you go off on a drunk for a couple of weeks every so often but don't touch a drop in between?"

"No. I've never gone off on a drunk in my life. Not for a couple of weeks or even a couple of days. And I rarely drink enough to get really drunk for more than it takes to sleep it off in one night."

She looked puzzled.

"I believe you. Funny thing, but because I believe you I think you better understand right now that I'm about ready to kill you. Are you aware of what you've been putting me through?"

She didn't expect any answer, for out came a torrent under great pressure, revealing the depth of her fury and humiliation.

"You've turned me inside out for months now. I thought I was losing my mind because I couldn't bring myself to believe you were losing yours. This goddamn road trip, the miserable audiences who expect Morticia and get Harold Pinter whom they don't understand,

and the small-town critics who think they do, have been enough to make me a gibbering idiot. But I can handle that. Now you, that's different. Do you have any idea what it took for me to ask another woman to come here, to see if you were alive? Yes, Natalie came here because I asked her to. I had a ghastly fear she might find you with somebody else. But then I thought . . . I mean . . . you read about the crime rate in New York, and people murdering people for pennies . . . and when they said the phone was off the hook I . . ."

Her voice broke as tears coursed down her cheeks. I started to rise, but she waved me away.

"No. Just stay away from me now. When Natalie called me back and said you looked like you were on some binge, I couldn't stand not knowing anymore. I had to find out for myself."

She reached into a box of Kleenex on the couch and blotted her face. Then, regaining control, she went on more quietly.

"I've said my piece. Now, tell me, for God's sake, what's wrong with you?"

I tried clearing my throat, but my breath got stuck. For the lack of any other ideas, I got to my feet, poked a finger into my vast gut and said:

"This."

Her expression turned a few somersaults before settling to a blank stare.

"What?"

I poked my bloated middle again and repeated:

"This."

"What do you mean, 'this'?"

"Just that. This."

"What 'this'?"

"This this!"

"Don't shout at me!" she snapped.

There was a slight pause. I tried again in a lower key.

"Didn't you notice it the instant I opened the door?"

"Notice what?"

I poked it again.

"This."

Carolyn's patience was on the verge of collapse, but she seemed to feel my waves of desperation.

"All right," she said, "let's start all over again. Now what was I supposed to notice the instant you opened the door?"

Why was she trying to be polite at a time like this, I wondered, pretending not to see that I looked like a blowfish? I angrily poked my finger at my middle and almost sank it clear up to my elbow.

"This," I gasped, losing air at a dangerous rate.

"Oh, no," she moaned, "we're not going into that idiot 'this' language again. Please, don't use the word 'this' for awhile. Or 'that' either. Just give me the name of the 'this' or the 'that.'"

Furious, because I was now utterly convinced she was trying to soothe me by pretense and guile, I jumped in place as high as I could in order to make my point. But a mere five inches of elevation in my bare feet only resulted in a pair of bone bruises.

"This, this, this," I howled in pain, poking myself like a madman, "means this." I stomped up and down the room, doing my best to break my arches. "Did you ever see a walking whale?"

I stopped smack in front of her. She had been watching my performance with shock turning to recognition, which gave way to something I could not have anticipated. Biting her lip, which I mistook to be a precaution against its trembling, she asked:

"You mean this?" She touched my protruding navel. "Is 'this' the 'this' that's been wrong with you?"

"Yes, that's . . . Oh Jesus! The shade!! The goddamn window shade is up! The whole world has got to be watching this . . . I mean that . . . ahh."

Stricken at the thought, I thundered to the window and began a *pas de deux* with a very stubborn shade. At last, when I'd just about given up, it submitted. But the minute I turned my back to resume my confession, it rolled up with a crackling slap. Feeling my veins snake to the surface, I headed for the john to get my bathrobe but stopped dead in my tracks at the sound of Carolyn's cloudburst of laughter.

With each attempt I made to find out what was so hysterically funny in addition to my bouncing belly, she pointed her finger, screeched the word "this" and was off on another shaking tear of uncontrollable laughter. During the couple of pauses she took to catch her breath, she managed to shriek:

"And to think . . . I've been saying . . . that bastard . . . when I should have said . . . this bastard . . ." and promptly collapsed, helpless to check her convulsions.

It didn't take any great insight to recognize she was laughing at something other than the sight of my belly. Or the ridiculous "this" routine we'd just been through. But at least she was blowing off steam with laughter rather than tears. Even if the joke was more of a nightmare, and on me. She had paid her first installment for the dubious privilege of having fallen in love with a fat man. She was unquestionably entitled to a few laughs, at the very least, for having made the initial investment.

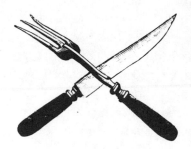

"Ideals such as honor, truth and respect weren't realized very much better in the past than they are today. But then, neither were they looked upon with scorn and cynicism. Where once these things were at least considered worthy, they are now dismissed as embarrassing affectations of a discredited heritage."

I nodded agreement with my eyes as the phrases of rolling rhetoric swept by me and out over the sea of shining faces behind me. I wondered about what might be behind the shine of all those faces. I also wondered what names belonged to each, although had I turned around to look, I would have recognized them all.

But at the moment, I felt their presence as the total of all the faces I had looked into during the past weeks since we had been in Beverly Hills. Hectic weeks, nerve-shattering weeks filled with so many comings and goings that I frequently mixed up my "Good evenings" and "Good nights" and had to be rescued by a gracious hostess or a watchful Carolyn.

Was it last week or the week before that Carolyn and I had arrived at a Masquerade Charity Ball amidst the click and flash of dozens of cameras? The exclusive guest list had not been restricted to the "who-was-still-who" of show business but also included a distinguished ambulatory representation of "who-had-been-who." In this hierarchy, I alone would not have rated an invitation and, in fact, received none. Carolyn was not only eligible, but a coveted guest.

Terrified at the prospect of mingling with such a collection of fame and beauty, I had tried every evasive maneuver in my repertoire when the invitation arrived.

"But I'm not known by many Hollywood people. So I'll feel like a fat idiot, and in a costume yet! I can see it now: Herb who? Any relation to Johnny Green?"

"Don't be ridiculous. Everybody is going to be too busy worrying about how they look, counting the autographs they're asked for in the lobby and wondering whether they were photographed as often as everybody else."

"But who can I come as? Fatty Arbuckle?"

"Look. You're making a mountain out of a molehill. Besides, I want to show you off. I want to say to the whole bunch: 'This is the man I choose. He's bright, kind, gentle, talented and very sexy!' "

"Well a lot of people may not quite see it that way."

"They'll learn."

I was pulled back to the present by some particularly fitting words.

". . . and it's a distortion of the truth to expose deep wounds. The test of truth lies in how true your feelings are for one another, so that you may bind up and heal deep wounds. Otherwise . . ."

That was a test, all right. And Carolyn passed and surpassed it many times over. And not by any pretense that ignored the facts. But rather by a clear perspective that never allowed my feelings about my overweight to be taken out of the context of the rest of who and what I was. Slowly, she was leading me to the threshold of that critical sense of proportion, which sharply divides self-laceration from self-criticism.

"O.K.," I had agreed, "but on one condition: First we get up a DFPL or D."

"I'll call Saks and order one in blue. Darling, what are you talking about?"

"DFPL or D: Distinguished Fat Persons Living or Dead list. If I'm going to get myself masqueraded up for a masquerade ball, I ought to masquerade as somebody who was somebody, not just any old nobody."

"Well, that should be easy enough. Let's see, there's Orson Welles, Charles Laughton, Walter Slezak, Thomas Gomez, Laird Cregar, Sidney Greenstreet. . . ."

"That's all inside stuff. Why not try naming a few famous hefties of history? The only big barrel I can think of is William Howard Taft. And who's going to scream: 'Why it's Vice President Teddy Roosevelt's running mate, President Taft, as I live and breathe!' "

"Don't be ridiculous. There are plenty to choose from."

"Name three."

"Well, there's Winston Churchill."

"No, baby, no. He was husky, stocky, but fat? Not on your life."

"Babe Ruth?"

"Nope. He was built out of round iron."

"Well, you've read a lot of history books. I'll bet you can name some very famous people who were overweight."

"Herman Göring. Nazi number two."

"Be serious."

In the end we had compromised. I'd come as Beethoven because I was crazy, a musician and had a lot of hair.

The resonant voice reclaimed my attention.

"Appearances are like the tip of an iceberg. While they shouldn't be ignored, it's a good thing to remember that you are only looking at ten percent of the whole. The remaining ninety percent that cannot be seen is the real size, weight and character of what you have to deal with."

Well, I wasn't so sure about that. I was thinking about the reference to appearances. I'd have given anything if my appearance in that waist-exposing Beethoven-style cutaway had only shown 10 percent of my pot. Pot? Hell. Double roaster superimposed on a bay window.

Carolyn had taken an infinity of pains for the occasion. Not only had I endured two fittings at Western Costume, whose professional reputation for authenticity was on the line, but she'd arranged for her make-up man, Norman Pringle, a magician with grease paint, to match my face with a famous portrait of the Great Master. I also had the experience of a motion picture hairdresser styling my mop *à la* the great Ludwig. But I had firmly declined to carry an ear trumpet—an instrument the deaf Beethoven had been obliged to use.

My Beethoven getup became such a project that I didn't get a chance to ask Carolyn about her own costume. I was downright indignant, therefore, when she emerged from her dressing room as the familiar, slinky Morticia Addams.

"No fair. Who's going to guess wrong about you except a few Chinese ping pong players?"

"Honey, I read a little bit about Mr. Beethoven to find out who his favorite person was and I don't think I'd look good as his nephew Karl. Morticia will have to do."

Our arrival at the Beverly Hilton had timed out with the arrival of several other crowd pleasers: Barbara Streisand, Omar Sharif and Sidney Poitier. The breathy oohs and aahs of the inevitable crowd of fans were punctured by the slam, slam of limousine doors.

I had pressed up as tight as I could to Carolyn's back in a frenzy to hide, and to hell with all appearances of decency. But her short, mincing steps, dictated by the narrowness of her costume, brought us to the brink of disaster almost immediately. My belly bumped her rear end and knocked her off balance. The crowd gasped as she teeter-tottered and only the lightning reflexes of the gallant Sidney Poitier saved her from a nasty spill. The crowd cheered and applauded.

"Thank you, Sidney. Whew! that was close," she said, kissing him on the cheek.

"Any time you feel like falling, Carolyn, my pleasure to catch you," he returned chivalrously, "any time at all."

"Oh, Sidney, I'd like you to meet . . ." Carolyn gestured to where I should have been, but was not. She peered into the darkness. "Darling? Darling? Where are you?"

I was where I had rebounded to as a result of the belly-to-butt collision: a few feet to the rear and frozen solid. As I thawed enough to waddle toward her, I heard a little kid in the crowd pipe up excitedly:

"That's Morticia! That's Morticia, Mommy! Why did that fat man push her like that?"

The voice in front of me suddenly stopped. The slight pause pulled me back once more and as I looked up, the rabbi caught my eye, smiled and continued.

"Herbert, do you take Carolyn . . ."

Six months of honeymooning blissed by. Carolyn's obvious and continuing happy state allayed my fear that one fine morning she'd waken and wonder what the hell I was doing there. Finding in many of her friends and acquaintances pungent examples of envy provided additional proof that something was definitely right with one Carolyn Jones Greene.

My last meeting with Skinny, with his recommendations to cool it, made even a deeper impression on me as the time passed, because Carolyn echoed them and then some. Although I kept nothing back about those agonizing months when she was on tour, I saw no wisdom in revealing my quaint relationship with Skinny. Why risk arousing even a tiny suspicion that I was hearing voices?

I even stabilized my weight. Instead of the eighty pounds of excess baggage I had been hauling around, I cut it to about fifty and leveled off. While this left me with enough unwanted poundage to curse myself for several times a day, I could admit I had eased down from the near-idiot-grotesque to the confirmed-stupid-obese.

But even that recrimination was vitiated by Carolyn's ingenuity and impeccable taste. Tactfully and patiently, she helped me to acquire a wardrobe of clever cut, color and design, which concealed what was not desirable by accenting what was. I would be astonished when catching a chance view of myself in a mirror, and almost succumb to the seduction. However, bathing was a corrective.

As a two-time matrimonial loser, I was naturally wary of connubial booby traps and tried to foresee as many as possible. However, I had few illusions that I could avoid all or even most of them. Here was where I could throw the full weight of my obesity into the balance and tilt the scales in favor of our marriage.

As is too well known, the first notes of marital discord strike insidiously. They appear in a slowly rising scale of sharp and flat tones of irritation. But I had a perfectly legitimate target for such pointed music.

Me.

My overweight.

My compulsion to gorge.

I resolved that whenever I felt a twinge of malice or spite, my obesity would be the bull's-eye. In that way, I could avoid inflicting most of the needless pinpricks on Carolyn and at the same time keep myself honest.

One night, as I lay awake reading, I was struck by a mordant phrase: "The trouble with age is that one had to have been young once to achieve it." I turned to look at Carolyn, peacefully asleep at my side. I wondered how much the nine-year difference between us showed. She looked, well, like Carolyn Jones, the sloe-eyed, sensuous beauty familiar to millions. Even without the make-up, the perfect hairdo, the rest of the artifice she used when facing the camera, she was a striking woman. Ageless, it seemed to me.

I got out of bed and tiptoed into her dressing room. I flicked the switch, and thirty light bulbs framing her full-length make-up mirror blazed on. I sat down to take a good look. No bad wrinkles, just three deep lines on my forehead, which gave the impression of intellect. No jowls, no puffiness, no telltale sag. Merely a hearty roundness without any special telling flaw. But the sum of all the details didn't seem to jibe with my actual years. I simply looked ten years older than forty-five. When added to the actual nine-year difference between my sleeping beauty and myself, that came unpleasantly close to twenty years. A generation.

I began to think about the greater longevity of women, added my nine years of seniority to that, wondered whether the extra ten in my appearance might not be something to be reckoned in also, and was overcome with sadness for my bride, who would be so prematurely widowed. The vision of her lonely days and nights overwhelmed me.

I slipped back into bed but couldn't shake off the dread and gloom. I tried to read and got nowhere. Sleep was out of the question. After an hour or so, the tension became unbearable. I shook Carolyn awake.

It wasn't easy, because she has the gift of deep sleep.

Persistence prevailed. When she finally opened her eyes, she asked, "What time is it?"

"Two thirty."

"Good night, darling." She closed her eyes contentedly.

"No, don't go back to sleep. Carolyn, Carolyn? Wake up, darling."

She stirred.

"What time is it?" she repeated.

"Two thirty."

"Two thirty? Why am I up?"

"I woke you."

"Oh, I see. Well, good night, darling."

"I'll only wake you again."

She sat up, yawning.

"Is something wrong?"

"I'm worried, Carolyn, very worried."

"Worried? What about?"

"About you."

"Me? Why?"

"The thought of you being a widow is killing me."

"Widow? What are you . . . honey, are you sick?"

"No. I'm not sick or anything like that. But you may be a widow soon."

Her eyes widened and she said in a small voice, "You're frightening me. What are you talking about?"

"Well, it's this. I owe you twenty years. And when you add that to the seven years of life expectancy that women have over men, that's twenty-seven years. Which means you'll be a widow much sooner than you have to unless you put me on a diet and take about ten years off the way I look."

Carolyn had been listening to me with the strained intensity usually observed only in the hard of hearing. When I finished, her immobility implied a concentrated effort to reconstruct every phrase in order to be certain that she hadn't distorted one word. Carolyn, fortunately, possesses total recall.

"What you want is for me to put you on a diet, is that right?"

"Yes."

"All right, darling, now go to sleep. I'll get some books and menus tomorrow. And no more crazy talk about making me a widow."

"It's not just crazy talk. There is a connection."

"What kind of connection?"

"Well, the other day, I was reading an ad for life insurance. The usual stuff. But it said something about meeting certain requirements about health. If you have any serious disease, forget it. One of the conditions is that if you are seriously overweight, they'll sell you a policy for three times as much as anybody else, and even reserve the right not to sell you a policy at all if you're over forty and seriously overweight. The odds are all against your living long enough to make the risk worth it to them."

Carolyn shuddered.

"I think you better see the doctor and find out if there's anything wrong."

"What for? There is something wrong. And there's nothing the doctor can do about it except to tell me to do something about it. Look, darling, the reason I woke you was to tell you that I feel terribly responsible. If I want to take the chance of dropping dead, I ought to do that alone. But we're married, and I don't have the right to inflict any of this on you. How would you like to have a bedridden, paralytic husband hanging around a couple of years? Well, with every day that passes, my chances get better I'll wind up that way unless I drop the weight and keep it off. I haven't been able to do it on my own. I have a feeling that with your help, I can make it. But it all starts with the fact that I have no right to expose you to the risks I run because I eat like a pig. Do you understand?"

Carolyn's face set in an expression I had seen only a few times but had come to recognize. Stubbornness held every feature rigid. Whenever she got that look, it was useless to try to budge her. Nothing on earth could deflect her from what she would do.

"I love you, darling. And if you're in any danger, so am I. I can't bear to think of anything happening to you. I feel responsible. When I found out just how important the overweight business was to you before we got married, I put it down to your feeling that I really didn't love the real you, but only the best-foot-forward-you. So I wanted to make it clear I loved you—fat or skinny. That it didn't matter. And you know, honey, it really doesn't. But your health and well-being does, so from now on, I'm going to be a tyrant."

Neither by nature nor inclination is Carolyn the type who'd voluntarily cook every day. But starting the next day, that's exactly what she did—and risked alienating our housekeeper, Marian, a splendid cook and very proud Scotswoman. Marian could be heard muttering from fifty feet away.

"Well, I never! You'd think I'd put poison in that muck. Back home, they'd all be saying I'd been told to buzz off and was being kept on as a charity case."

However, Carolyn had made her decision and no amount of sulking or dark hints and threats from Marian could change it. Carolyn explained that she was learning how to prepare low-calorie dishes and that once she had, she would instruct Marian in the art of low-calorie gourmet cooking.

Carolyn interrupted work on her novel and turned down one picture and two TV dramatic shows in order to get the weight-control program going. Not only did she fix three meals per day, but also a variety of mid-morning and late-afternoon snacks.

My portions were carefully weighed and measured, and she watched me like a hawk to make certain I ate every morsel.

"You must finish this, darling, because the nutrition is carefully figured out. Also, this will keep you from being hungry, so you won't be tempted to overeat."

I was so touched by the concern and devotion she showed in fussing endless hours with complicated recipes that I obeyed to the letter. She was very proud to bring me a late-afternoon snack of "roasted peanuts" made of baked mushrooms and canapés consisting of whipped low-fat cottage cheese on paper-thin wafers.

Not content with simply cooking dietetic meals, Carolyn insisted they pass her own rigid taste standards. Many a day, she cooked and threw out two or even three dinners because, she said, "It tastes like boiled rabbit dung."

Three weeks passed. Then, one night Carolyn said:

"Darling, I know we agreed not to look at the scale for a month. You said you'd like to see a big drop instead of pound or half-pound daily dribbles. But you look so much thinner. Can't we have the fun of seeing it tonight?"

The wistful way in which she asked was irresistible. So we went into the bathroom and I got on the scale. Carolyn jumped with excitement.

"Darling! Fifteen pounds! I did it! I took fifteen pounds off you. All that onion peeling was worth it! Oh, darling, I'm so happy."

So was I. Happy for the loss and happy for her. She began washing her face and fussing with oils and cleansers. I could see her eyes dancing excitedly. When she was through, she casually stepped on the scale herself. And let out an awesome shriek.

"Oh my God. Oh no! I've gained your goddamn fifteen pounds!"

I looked. It was true. I couldn't understand it.

"But how did you do it on diet food?" I asked, stunned.

"I've been tasting food all week long to make sure it's right. I couldn't bring myself to throw out all the stuff that came out lousy. So I ate it. Oh God, look at those hips," she wailed. "You must be revolted."

I put my arms around her. She sobbed:

"How can you even touch me?"

Within ten days Carolyn shed the fifteen pounds. The disgust she exhibited when she first made the discovery remained with her until every excess ounce was gone. It took another week of stepping on the scale three or four times a day before she finally accepted the fact that everything was back to normal.

If she could feel so strongly about her measly fifteen pounds, what must she really be feeling about my extra baggage? The answer lay so far beyond my courage that I hysterically wiped out both question and answer the instant they occurred.

This led to a new turn in my attitude toward Carolyn. I resented the way she supervised my meals. Her painstaking care, her diligence in measuring out my portions began to irritate me. I suspected her of deliberately cheating on the amount: cutting and trimming an ounce here, a spoonful there, withholding a few sticks of carrots or splitting the celery stalks in half so that I wouldn't notice the deception. I was certain she was checking the food inventory each day to entrap me. My irritability grew to a barely concealed fury.

My slow weight loss stalled and went into reverse. I managed this by midnight raids on the ice cream in the freezer. I ignored the scale pointedly and watched Carolyn fight down constant impulses to ask questions. Tense silences cooled our relationship considerably. Silences I shattered with violent outbursts at the ills of everybody and everything in the world. At first she tried to be conciliatory, but tiring of my unvarying negatives, began to retort tartly and ended up withdrawing behind a barricade of icy formality. Our reconciliations merely raised the temperature of our relationship from zero to the freezing point.

It was clear this couldn't go on indefinitely. Nevertheless, many weeks slipped by that saw our formerly happy home transformed to opposing wings of an armed camp. The longer the build-up continued, however, the more reluctant each of us felt about firing the first shot.

One morning, as I struggled with a piece of music that stubbornly resisted my attempts at resolution, Carolyn knocked at my studio door. "Well, come in," I grated uninvitingly.

She pretended not to notice.

"I'm sorry for interrupting, but I wanted to tell you we're having guests tonight."

"Who?" I asked, making it clear I already resented them, whoever they might be.

"Dr. Warren Stuart and his wife."

"Who is Dr. Stuart and wife?"

She swallowed that one but didn't quite manage to keep a trace of strain from her voice.

"He'll be lecturing at tomorrow night's meeting of the Thalians. Since it's my turn to be chairlady, I thought I should get acquainted with him first."

"The Thalians?" I asked blankly. "Oh, the Thalians. Isn't that the outfit where civilians and show biz folk rub shoulders and raise money for kids or something?"

"The something is why we raise money for kids. Emotionally disturbed kids. Which I've told you all about dozens of times. Dr. Stuart is one of the country's leading authorities on the subject. He's the head of an experimental school and clinic in Chicago. It should be an interesting evening."

"I'll bet," I muttered.

"You'll bet what?" Carolyn flared up dangerously.

"I'll bet it will be interesting," I backed off lamely.

She stared into and through me. Then her manner shifted, suggesting first things first.

"Cocktails at seven, dinner at seven-thirty. Marian is off today. I was hoping you'd help me."

"O.K."

She nodded and turned to go. I wanted to put an end to our war of nerves, but where to begin?

"Er, I'm sorry I sounded like the house Dracula," I mumbled.

She stopped and faced me. Her eyes no longer smoldered, but seemed wary.

"That's O.K. I guess I was a little salty too."

She waited for me to say something. Not knowing how to continue, I turned to the piano.

"It's this damn hunk of music. It starts out like a dream. Then it begins chasing itself."

She nodded encouragingly.

"See? It's good, damn good so far," I spoke through the music, "but right here, it begins to fade. Do you hear how it can't make up its mind to go up or go down or stay put or. . . ."

The telephone on my desk jangled. Carolyn got to it before the second ring.

"Hello? Oh yes. I'll wait."

She shrugged her shoulders apologetically, covered the phone and said, "The Thalians Committee. They want to introduce Dr. Stuart to me."

"Well, dammit to hell," I exploded. "Why didn't they think of that before interrupting fifty times a day and . . ."

"Yes? Oh, hello, Dr. Stuart. No, no, you're not disturbing me at all." She waved me to silence as she spoke. After a few pleasantries and a hasty confirmation of the seven o'clock date, she was through. It all took only fifteen or twenty seconds, but the moment was gone.

"I'm sorry," she said. "Now where do you think the music starts wandering?"

"Ahh, never mind. I'll beat the son of a bitch into shape or torture it till it dies."

I began banging the piano in the middle of the critical phrase and simply kept repeating the same few notes while I cursed. After the third or fourth time around I sensed Carolyn leave the studio. A bare suggestion of the latch click told me what I already knew: The door was closed again.

I stopped beating on the piano and experienced a strange phenomenon. A storm of sounds broke within me, a jumble of everything I had ever heard in my life. Among them were the quickly repeated chimes of crowded old-time trolley cars, the cooing of fat-breasted pigeons in the park, the gear grinding of squat old automobiles, the heavy impact of the Philharmonic finishing Beethoven's Fifth Symphony, the wide-barreled guns along the Rhine and the riveting on the hull of a broad-beamed man-of-war in an old newsreel. An infinity of sounds, remembered sounds, made-up sounds, all disappearing and reappearing like so many compatible liquids in a steaming vat, each one having its split second of recognition as it boiled up, burst its bubble and dropped back to the din within the cauldron.

The lightest touch of a single note on the piano acted like a circuit breaker, as one fragile sound shut off the whirling vibrations in my head. I heard only what I played, but the moment I stopped, the inner roar resumed. Suddenly, the sounds grew dimensions other than acoustical. They took on succulent fragrances, irresistible tempting shapes and mouth-watering tastes. The moment I recognized I had converted the food of the spirit to the food of the flesh, I slammed the piano shut in disgust.

"**A**ctually, we're still in the Middle Ages as far as preventing or curing the miseries of emotionally disturbed children," Dr. Warren Stuart was saying as we sipped our after-dinner coffee in the library.

"Do you see much obesity in emotionally disturbed children?" I asked.

"No, not very much, But we've got some cases."

"Do you find anything special about that? I mean, are there any personality patterns in these kids that are distinctive?" I pressed.

"No. We haven't noticed anything special or unique in obese children."

"Are you able to cure the fat kids?" I asked.

Out of the corner of my eye, I saw Carolyn begin to fidget. She shot a worried look at me.

"I'm afraid that curing disturbed youngsters is a long way off, as I said."

"If you're wondering whether we are successful

with their weight problems, Mr. Greene," Mrs. Stuart said, going to the heart of the matter, "the answer is yes—but. Yes, if they are living at the school. But no, if they are living at home."

"Is that any different from the way other children react?" Carolyn asked almost defensively. Now she avoided my eyes.

"No, no, not the least," Dr. Stuart said. "We often see a child who has made great progress retreat back into the old destructive patterns after a weekend at home."

The Stuarts were an easy-going, charming couple in their early fifties. Unpretentious, down to earth and very much absorbed in their work. And they were refreshingly direct and straightforward, as their unselfconscious response to my pointed question proved. We were soon on a first-name basis.

Without quite knowing it, I found myself irresistibly driven to talk about obesity with them. Not that I hoped they could help me to understand my own difficulties any better, nor was I looking for some abracadabra or formula for instant slenderhood. No, I was too old a hand at the fat racket now. But something I had once thought or heard was buzzing around in my head. Something about my being only half crazy, and in order to help myself I had to find the other half and put both halves together.

Suddenly the thought burst through with great clarity and triggered the reason why I needed to talk with these two people. I wanted, no, needed to prove to them I was insane on the subject of food. Then I would prove that they, meaning the medical profession, were insane in their treatment of obesity.

"Well," I began, fighting my impulse to shoot the works in one blast, "it looks like the fat problem is no easier to beat in emotionally disturbed kids than in us grownups."

"Possibly," Warren Stuart said. "After all, it's difficult to deal with an unstable child but one can reason with an adult."

"Reason?" I laughed, somewhat incredulously, indicating my girth.

"There are many more factors than reason, of course." Warren smiled. "Motivation, the desire to change habit patterns, the change of self-image and so on. When these factors are understood, the person changes."

"I wonder. It seems to me that all the psychological insight, all the medical knowledge and all the nutritional expertise are missing the point."

"What do you mean, Herb?" Christina Stuart asked with genuine interest. "How does all this expertise miss the point?"

"Well, we've all finished a lovely dinner, thanks to my wife. Could any of you eat another one right now?"

The Stuarts shook their heads. So did Carolyn.

"But I could. And I ate more than any of you. I was watching."

Carolyn shredded a Kleenex.

"Would anybody care for more coffee?" she asked desperately.

I waited through the polite refusals.

"Please forgive me, but I was watching myself mainly. When I watched you, it was only to try to understand something about sanity in food."

"Sanity in food? What do you mean?" Warren asked.

"Look at the four of us. Three are not fat. One is. Me. I eat too much. So I watched the portions you all took and tried to take about the same. I couldn't."

"What do you mean, couldn't?" Christina asked.

"I kept debating whether my helpings were the same or a little less. Your plates looked filled. My plate looked empty. So I added a bit of this and that. In the end, I had double the amount of any of you."

"When did you become aware that you had twice as much as any of us?" Warren wanted to know.

"Oh, when I was about half-way through."

"In that case, why didn't you stop eating?"

"I tried. But I wasn't even certain it was really half. So I had a bit more just to be sure. Then I noticed I was way over the half. At that point, I felt there was no sense trying the impossible, I might just as well finish it off."

There was a pause while the Stuarts digested that. Carolyn was past describing.

"Wait a minute," Warren said, puzzled. "I still don't understand why you couldn't stop eating when you were half-way through."

"Because I felt so utterly defeated. And to top it off, I got even more confused because I felt a pang of hunger."

"More likely a cramp of protest from a full belly."

"Dead center, Warren. That's another thing I can't judge until it's too late."

Christina Stuart took over.

"Since you can't judge these things yourself, Herb, why not have someone else judge for you?"

I turned to Carolyn. Her color showed pasty under her makeup. But now that I had launched this thing, there was no turning back.

"Darling," I said to my long-suffering wife, "you can answer that one."

The Stuarts turned to her expectantly. Carolyn gulped but gamely went through with it.

"We tried that for awhile. It only worked for a short time, I'm afraid. It was my fault. I just couldn't bear being Herb's conscience any more."

I almost lost my courage, but I had to tell my wife the truth. Even if it was in front of strangers.

"It wasn't her fault at all," I said. "I had no business making her act as my conscience to begin with. But the real reason it didn't work was because I became suspicious that my wife was short-changing my portions."

Another look at my stricken bride almost finished me. I turned to a less personal facet of the story.

"There was also the food scale. I could hardly get paranoid about that. But I could and did begin to regard it as a tyrant dictating to me how much I might eat, just as I regarded the clock as a monster determining when I might eat. And when I disobeyed both for any period of time, the bathroom scale entered the picture to make the final judgment. You see, Christina,

I felt I was being run by a mere collection of screws and bolts, so I simply rebelled and said to hell with the diet."

Christina nodded wryly.

"Herb, I know you are not being facetious at our expense, you're not merely trying to make the case that nothing works, so what is it you're trying to establish?"

I could have kissed her. She had given me the cue I needed.

"I believe that the whole approach to the problem of obesity by the medical profession is as insane as the obese person's approach is to food. That's what I think I can establish."

"And how do you propose to go about that?" Warren smiled indulgently.

"Mind you," Christina said engagingly, "we doctors as individuals are just as crazy as anybody else. We're human too. But you're questioning a method, not a person or group of persons. Wouldn't you say?"

"Yes, of course. And I'll need your help. You're a pair of distinguished researchers, you know the discipline and the rules of proof. If both of you could help me prove that by all accepted clinical standards, I am insane where food is concerned, it would be a first step. Will you help me?"

Dr. Stuart turned to his wife.

"What do you say, Chris? Why don't we test him for the classic signs of insanity?"

"All right," she said. "But let's agree that this is restricted to food," she added with a smile.

"Agreed," I said, sneaking a look at Carolyn.

She leaned forward, apparently no longer embarrassed.

The Stuarts showered me with questions.

"How often do you think about food?"

"It's a constant companion. Many times every day."

"Are these thoughts about food pleasant?"

"Yes. But that's always wrecked by anxiety, guilt and worry."

"Have you ever been successful at losing weight?"

"Yes. So many times, that the grand total must be thousands of pounds."

"Did you think of food the same way during those times?"

"Absolutely. If anything, more so."

"Do you know you may literally kill yourself with food?"

"Certainly."

"Are you ever free from worrying one way or another about food?"

"Never. Absolutely never."

"Do you think of food as poison?"

"No. I think the way I use it is poisonous."

"Have you gotten medical and psychiatric advice and treatment?"

"Several times."

"And after having failed with professional help, did you blame the doctors?"

"At first. But when I got right down to it, I did the eating, not the doctors."

"How did you regard the doctors?"

"At best, arrogant ignoramuses. At worst, sordid frauds."

"Have you ever met anybody who understands your problem?"

"I never met a slender person who did. I don't believe they exist. I never discussed it with other obese people. They revolt me."

"Do you think any accepted authorities in the field might have something useful for you?"

"I've read all the authorities. They're simply repetitive. And those working on the hereditary theory of obesity are going to have one hell of a time explaining why the genes waited in some cases for forty or fifty years before infecting their owners with fat. Imagine: forty or fifty years of sane food behavior and then, zap! The genes go beserk!"

"Do you feel all alone in this?"

"Yes. I feel, well, I feel as though I'm all alone in the world of zoo keepers."

"How do you mean?"

"I feel watched, laughed at, ridiculed and judged by everybody. Even by other obese people. I feel they all think I belong in a zoo. And the worst part of it is that I agree. Except that the rest of the world also belongs in a zoo."

"Why?"

"Just because I'm condemned to put my greed on display doesn't mean that I have a monopoly on greed. I'm inclined to think that the less obvious greed may be a worse form and deserve greater punishment."

The couple stopped for a moment. Then Dr. Stuart said, "Well, here it is, Chris. Obsessive, irrational, suspicious, hostile, potentially violent, suicidal, compulsive, paranoid, circular, unreasoning, depressed, masochistic, excessively harsh in self-judgment, incapable of choice, inability to distinguish between real or imagined injury or insult, aware of self-perpetuation of danger to life but unable to avert it. Fanatic insistence that nobody in the world but himself knows anything about the trouble. Diagnosis: insanity with respect to food."

Christina made a face.

"If you went on a diet, all of this would be academic. A diet is clearly the indicated therapy," she said patiently.

"True enough," I replied, "but obviously, that doesn't quite work. If you were obese, you would understand why."

"Surely you're not suggesting that a doctor must have a disease before he can cure it?" she asked sharply.

"No, of course not."

"Well, you've convinced my husband that you are insane on the subject of food. Insanity is a disease, Herb."

"Quite right. But obesity is more than a disease. It's a life style. And that's what none of you medical people comprehend. The obese speak a foreign language to you and you might as well be speaking in gobbledegook for all the sense you make to fat people."

Dr. Stuart showed signs of irritation. His voice dried out and he gesticulated excessively.

"Foreign language, Mr. Greene? We've all understood the words used here this evening."

"No, Dr. Stuart, you're wrong. Yours is the skinny language. I speak in fat. We said the word hunger.

You know what you feel when you use the word hunger. But you said I confused it with something else. Why confine my confusion to one word? There's every reason to suppose you don't know what I feel about words like handsome man, attractive man, gentle man or any other kind of man, including fat man."

"Oh, come now. It doesn't require great imagination to understand that some people are self-conscious about their looks," he protested.

"Can you say you understand the word dancing the way fat people do?" I asked. "Or ice skating? How about swimming, Dr. Stuart? But before swimming, try bathing suit for size and compare it with a fat man's version."

"I think I can do that," Dr. Stuart said, "and I don't find myself struggling with a foreign language. Merely another set of painful symptoms of a specific disorder. You're talking about a semantic difference, not another language."

"You say semantics, I say that fat language implies much more. Take temptation, for example. What can you know of the word temptation as fat people experience it? We're not tempted by food, Dr. Stuart, we simply devour it whenever we wish and whenever we don't wish. But lots of fat people are tempted by other things, such as love affairs, believe it or not. And to be tempted by a tempting person, Dr. Stuart, but to feel that you yourself are about as tempting as a beached whale, is quite a temptation in itself. Almost irresistible, every time out. So that if, by some miracle, a tempting person is tempted by you—you, who know yourself to offer nothing worthwhile in the way of temptation—you suspect the tempting person of some awful perversion, ready to use you to practice on. Isn't that a foreign use of language at the very least? Foreign enough to assume it goes hand in hand with the life style it expresses?

"Yes, Dr. Stuart, there is a fat language. And also a fat life style. The fat experience, if you will, encompasses fat laughter, fat tears, fat regret, fat love, fat frustration, fat misery and fat everything else about which you know nothing.

"But you, and I mean all the medical you, presume to diagnose, treat and cure. How would you go about curing a life style in the first place? The very idea sounds insane. More than that, it is insane. Which is what I set out to establish. I'm insane on the subject of food, and the medical profession is equally insane in the treatment of obesity."

I had intended to follow up with an alternative: the clear-cut way out of the jungle of obesity. But the disturbed atmosphere was only inducive to a quiet but quick parting of the Stuarts and the Greenes. Besides, what I had grasped was still only theory. I now needed to demonstrate it.

After waving goodnight to our guests, Carolyn and I remained wordless at the front door.

"Well," I said finally, "we might as well start clearing up the mess."

Without a flicker of acknowledgment, Carolyn headed toward the dining room. The dregs of food on the plates, the half-carved roast, the salad bowl of slick drooping greens, the half-empty wine and water glasses, all the usual remnants littered the table. She eyed it with a peculiar feverish look.

I reached for a plate to begin the stacking and carting but was stopped by a piercing cry from my wife.

"No! Don't! Oh, excuse me. Maybe there's a different word for don't in your language."

She shuddered in much the same way a wet cat dries itself.

"It's not every woman who can boast that she married a man without even noticing that he speaks a foreign language. I mean, it is rather quaint to say 'Darling, I love you,' and not know your husband may think it means 'Have some more potatoes.' Very quaint."

She viciously kicked off her shoes. One skittered across the floor and knocked over a plant by the window. The other did a high loop and divebombed the gravy boat, which was unfortunately close to her. The fallout impartially splattered the tablecloth and Carolyn's white pants suit. She didn't blink an eye.

"I've been trying to translate lots of things you've said to me. I imagine some of them are very funny. Little things like when we make love and you say 'delicious, I want more.' I can only guess what that must mean. Does it gain a little something in the translation? I'm just beginning to understand a word here and there. But when I think of the killing laughs I've missed, I can hardly wait until I figure out a few more words. Or maybe you'll explain the choicer bits as we go along. Then we can both die laughing.

"But maybe I'm being too hard on you. This language barrier between us is my fault. Really, it's all my fault, I should have realized it a long time ago. I should have tried to learn it. But better late than never, I always say. Well, I can't stuff myself the way you do in order to join your club. But there's more than one way to skin a cat."

She dug into the hollandaise sauce and began rubbing it over her hands.

"Am I doing this right, Herbert? I know this is a crazy way of getting food, but being crazy is your specialty. You proved that tonight. Oh dear, I'm afraid the sauce isn't quite getting through."

She tugged at her pants suit zipper, which got stuck. After a brief struggle, she reached for a greasy carving knife and simply hacked herself loose. Tossing aside the shredded blouse and pants, she ripped off her bra and panties. Stark naked, she faced me with a look that could have stared down the demonic eye of Moby Dick.

She grabbed a handful of butter and a handful of cranberry sauce, smearing her face and arms.

"Ah, that's better, wouldn't you say, Herbert? You're the expert on this."

Grabbing at everything in sight, she went on plastering herself without interrupting her running monologue.

"How'm I doing? I think I'm beginning to get the feel of this. Say something in fat. Come on, anything. I betcha a handful of horseradish sauce I'll understand you better now.

"And you have a right to an understanding wife. When I think of all the months and months you had to put up with my idiotic ignorance, when all the time your heart was breaking because I misunderstood everything you said or did, I could die of shame."

She picked up the slab of beef, bit into it, chewing furiously. She swallowed a solid lump but coughed it up in the nick of time. Shrugging, she tossed the beef away.

"That wasn't very good. But be patient, you poor misunderstood man, I need a little more practice."

Her voice broke. She tried to go on, but a terrible sob stopped her. But only for a moment.

"I know the secret. I know how to understand you. I've got to get it all through my head first."

She picked up the salad bowl and turned it over on her head. Wilted greens slid and dripped past her face, over her shoulders and down her back and breasts. Then she collapsed, no longer capable of choking back her tears. As she sank to the floor, the large salad bowl fell off her head and rolled around to a noisy stop. Sitting like a twisted doll, she wracked out her misery.

I unfroze and sat down beside her. I put my arms around her and held her close. And cried with her. After great heavings and wailings, we cried ourselves out. She dropped her head to my shoulder, and I dropped mine to hers. A piece of lettuce that had stuck to her skin tickled my nose. Not wanting to let go of her, I flicked it off with my tongue. I held her tight and whispered, "Honey?"

"Yes?"

"There's too much vinegar in the salad dressing."

The next morning, I set out my theory on a half-dozen typed sheets. Then I tried explaining to my victimized wife.

"Darling, any apology I could make for all the misery I've caused you would sound like a worn-out record. What counts is action. Starting now, I handle my food problem by knocking off the weight and keeping it off without turning your life upside down. That means you behave exactly as though I have no problem at all. No more complicated menus or diets for you to dream up. No more special attitudes or behavior. O.K.?"

"But we live together. And we eat most meals together." She hesitated. "I don't understand."

"I think I've discovered a new wrinkle about overweight. It has to do with why diets don't work for compulsive eaters."

Carolyn looked pained.

"But you just said you'd knock off weight and keep it off. How can you do that without going on a diet?"

"By instituting a cycle that automatically elim-inates the self-destruct mechanisms built into all re-ducing diets, which are the reasons why diets don't work for compulsive eaters."

"That sounds like a lot of fancy talk to me. What-ever you eat is your diet, whether you call it a cycle or anything else."

I didn't expect her to be convinced by words. Be-sides, there were too many false starts in my history.

"Suppose we do this by the week. Then you can see what I'm doing, how a cycle differs from a diet, and most important, whether it works. At the end of each week, I'll give you a new cycle and we can talk about it." I handed her one of the typed pages. "Here's Cycle One."

	BREAKFAST	LUNCH	DINNER
Monday	½ grapefruit Coffee, tea or water	3 oz. cottage cheese, Coffee, tea or water	½ broiled chicken breast without skin Mixed green salad without dressing Coffee, tea or water
Tuesday	"	"	"
Wednesday	"	"	"
Thursday	"	"	"
Friday	"	"	"
Saturday	"	"	"
Sunday	Liquid diet all day		

She read it through and was silent for a while.

"But how are you going to feel? Won't you be starving all the time?"

"Let's try to handle this a week at a time. After this cycle is over, we can talk about it. Also the scale will tell us how it's working."

At first she wanted to share some of my austerity because she felt she might be tempting me or that I was suffering great hardship. I repeatedly had to insist that she not curtail the variety or amount of her own eating because of me. If she wanted dessert, she was to have it. In fact, I was at pains to point out that the success of the experiment was strongly tied to the free play she gave to her own behavior. In this case, her appetite.

While she honored our bargain to wait until the week was over before talking about my new theory, she barely made it.

"You dropped eight pounds and I'm very happy about it. But isn't this a very hard way to lose weight? Don't you have awful hunger pangs?"

"Hunger pangs don't last very long. Besides, anybody who claims that losing weight is easy is a goddamn liar. Nothing worthwhile is easy. All those commercials and it-won't-hurt-eat-what-you-want-and-lose-ugly-fat diets are a fraud. A fat person can't eat what he wants and still lose weight. Take me, for instance."

"Doesn't it take terrific willpower all day long?"

"No. First of all, willpower isn't turned on like water from a faucet. So it doesn't have to be under constant pressure. Secondly, if willpower is involved, everybody has plenty to spare. Think of all the unpleasant don'ts and do's people live with every day of their lives. They don't cave in except once in a while, which is human. Most people don't quit jobs when they get fed up or reject surgery when they're sick; they don't shoot the mayor because they can't sue city hall. And they don't refuse to do all those necessary but miserable things that require what's called willpower."

She looked skeptical. So I tried another tack.

"Honey, when you're shooting a picture, don't you have days when you want to tell everybody to eat arsenic on their way to hell? Aren't there days you'd trade your place in heaven just to be alone instead of making love to the camera?"

"More times than I can remember."

"Well, why don't you do it?"

"Oh well, my pride is involved. And I have a responsibility to all the other people working. My professional ethics, my reputation are on the line. Then, there's a sense of discipline, a feeling of accomplishment. Things like that."

"Do you use terrific willpower thinking all these things every minute of the day?"

"I don't have to. These things are part of me. Like my hands, my face, my whole being."

"And how do you feel when somebody says that you actors have it easy? That all you have to do is make faces?"

"Sometimes I want to scream. Mostly, I feel they don't know what they're talking about."

I paused. She started to say something once or twice but stopped herself. Something clicked into place.

There was no need to say any more about willpower or the discomfort of hunger pangs. I handed her Cycle II.

	BREAKFAST	LUNCH	DINNER
Monday	½ grapefruit Coffee, tea or water	3 oz. cottage cheese, Coffee, tea or water	Poached salmon, Cooked broccoli Coffee, tea or water
Tuesday	"	"	"
Wednesday	"	"	"
Thursday	"	"	"
Friday	"	"	"
Saturday	"	"	"
Sunday	Liquid diet all day		

Everything proceeded smoothly until Friday afternoon. I had just finished scoring a TV private eye movie and was having a cup of coffee. Carolyn came in after taping a week of shows for "Password."

I kissed her hello and asked, "How'd it go, honey? Was it fun?"

"Oh fine, it was fine," she answered flatly.

That didn't sound right. Carolyn loves to play Password and is so good at it that she is regularly invited back.

"Something go wrong?" I asked.

"No. All the shows went well."

"Something's not going well. What's wrong?"

She looked perfectly miserable.

"I feel terrible. Grace and Harold Robbins are giving a dinner party tonight. The invitation came three weeks ago. And I simply forgot all about it."

"Well, you've got plenty of time to get ready, and I don't think we got a better offer tonight. So why do you feel terrible?"

"You're wonderful," she said, "just wonderful," as though I was some kind of a shining knight in shinier armor.

"I don't get it, honey. Why do you feel you're Mrs. Terrible and I'm Mr. Wonderful?"

"Darling, you don't have to keep up such a beautiful front. We'll figure a way out together."

This was definitely not illuminating. And it was getting a little scary too.

"Look, honey, the only wonderful thing I did today was maybe three and a half bars of that Private Eyewash stuff I just finished. And my front ain't really beautiful yet and it kind of keeps up by itself anyway. So what is the terrible feeling you have about the Robbinses' dinner party, which they don't have to know you forgot about anyway, and that we'll figure a way out of together?"

"Your cycle. If we go to that damn dinner party, it'll ruin your salmon-broccoli cycle. I feel terrible. Maybe we could take a piece of fish and a flower or two of broccoli over to Grace's? That would work, wouldn't it?"

I must have laughed for an hour. Then I told her, "Don't worry about carting a doggy bag because I figured social possibilities into my cycle."

"But how are you going to diet, I mean cycle, at a party?"

"Darling, listen. It's no skin off anybody else's ass if I decide to drop some lard from mine. Remember we agreed that you were not going to get sympathy pangs because you thought I might be hungry. So what makes you think a pack of half-stoned show business-niks are going to go on a sympathy food strike even if they knew what I was up to? Do a bunch of drunks at a party stop drinking because an alcoholic is around sipping ginger ale? Trust me, honey. We can talk about it after we get home. But let's have a good time tonight. What do you say? The Robbinses always throw a good bash."

Several hours later we were in the midst of a herd of show folk at the Robbinses' elegant home. The booze and people flowed like booze and people generally do. Carolyn was more nervous than a black widow on her wedding night as we performed the hello-darling alley-ritual of cheek-to-cheek greetings with old friends, while wasting empty lip kisses upon the Southern California desert air.

An army of floating waiters were bobbing up all over the place offering drinks and hors d'oeuvres. I stopped one and turned to Carolyn.

"What'll you have, honey?"

"Oh, I don't know," she said uncertainly.

"I know what I'm drinking, so take your pick before the man goes."

Her eyes widened in fright.

"A double Scotch and soda," she gulped and looked terrified as she waited to hear what I was going to order.

"Make mine a triple water over ice, please."

The waiter blinked, unsure he had heard right.

"A triple vodka, sir?"

"No. Water. Plain old vanilla water. I'm an alcoholic, waiter," I added confidentially.

A wave of sympathy almost swamped him.

"Yes, sir. Right away," he breathed dramatically, certain that if I didn't get my water fix immediately, I'd resume my wicked alcoholic ways and he'd be responsible.

Carolyn cracked up as she watched my self-appointed savior execute a great broken-field run through the crowd.

"He's going to stick closer to you than Dr. Kildare to Gillespie to make sure you don't give in to temptation. Oh, here comes Grace."

After we helloed and how-are-you-ed and started some chit-chat, the waiter returned.

"Your Scotch, Miss Jones." He bowed graciously to Carolyn and then, with a wink that could be seen from an off-shore drilling site in the Gulf of Mexico, he said, "Your vodka, sir."

"Thank you," I said pleasantly and pinched my ready-to-explode wife. Fortunately, the waiter's winking eye was not in Grace Robbins' line of sight, and the great water conspiracy sprang no leak.

Dinner passed according to my cycle plan for parties. Three spoonfuls or forkfuls of whatever was served, with the exception of any creamed gooed-up food or dessert, which was fine because three bites of melon plus three bites of roast beef, three shots of string beans and three speared pieces of salad stopped my discomfort before it could really bug me. The magic number was three. No more than three. Less, if the feeling of nobility was so great as to make me lose my head.

The party adjourned to the plush, cushioned furniture of the living room for dessert and coffee. And it was there that I encountered the only obstacle in the course of the evening. Carolyn and I were comfortably ensconced on a sofa and exchanging shop talk in that slow after-dinner rhythm with some others who felt like it. A well-turned-out lady floated into the group and enthusiastically announced:

"Wait until you see that divine pastry. It's simply heavenly. Ah, there it is. You mustn't miss it. It's the best thing of its kind ever. I've just got to see your faces when you bite into it. You'll flip."

"How would you know that, Elaine?" someone asked. "They only just brought it in. Did you sneak into the kitchen and taste it?"

"Taste it, hell! I baked it."

Elaine insisted upon serving it to the little group. As I happened to be seated on the fringe, I was the last one of about ten guests. I saw Carolyn tense up as Elaine approached us with two plates. Carolyn took her plate and hoped for the best.

"Thank you," I said politely, "but I simply can't."

Clearly Elaine was so used to getting her own way that she didn't even register my refusal.

"You look like a man who can't wait for the dessert," she said, extending the plate.

"Thank you, but I'd rather not," I said.

She looked amazed.

"But you can't refuse."

"Well then, let's say I don't refuse but I respectfully decline," I feebly joked.

"Why?" she demanded.

Fortunately, my cycle plan for parties also covered unlikely stupidities committed by dummies.

"I'm allergic to whipped cream." The magic word allergy repeated a few times would do the trick.

"Oh, that's no problem. The topping is sculptured sugar frosting. It only looks like whipped cream."

"I'm also allergic to frosting. Really, I break out like mad."

For a moment she was stumped. But she got a flash.

"Well, I'll remove the frosting. It's the pastry that's wild. Really wild."

"I know this sounds nuts, but I'm also allergic to pastry."

I felt Carolyn about to say something, but I squeezed her hand in restraint. After all, the battle was over.

But Elaine was as resourceful as a Jewish mother feeding her only son on the first Friday night dinner after his honeymoon.

"Well, I got the answer. The last layer is brandied fruit. I'll just remove it and you won't have to worry about your allergies."

Embarrassment was rife in the little group. I was more than a little hot under the collar.

"Elaine," I said, "I don't know you and you don't know me. But why are you pushing the pastry so hard? Something wrong with it?"

"Wrong with it? I advise you to taste it before you say something's wrong with it."

At this point, Carolyn stepped in. "You're on dangerous ground. My husband often gives people scatological advice for food disposal."

"What's that?"

"That means," someone piped up, "stick it up your ass."

Elaine was astonished, but replied:

"Well why didn't he say so? I can take a hint."

The last two days of the second cycle passed without further adventure. The scale registered a seven-pound drop. I handed over Cycle III.

	BREAKFAST	LUNCH	DINNER
Monday	½ grapefruit Coffee, tea or water	3 oz. cottage cheese, Coffee, tea or water	1 lean broiled lamb chop, ⅓ cup cooked string beans, ½ sliced tomato, Coffee, tea or water
Tuesday	"	"	"
Wednesday	"	"	"
Thursday	"	"	"
Friday	"	"	"
Saturday	"	"	"
Sunday	Liquid diet all day		

Upon completion of Cycle III, another seven pounds went the way of unwelcome flesh. Carolyn was curious.

"Darling, I don't want to throw a hex on this, but wouldn't you do as well on a strict reducing diet figured out by a doctor and nutritionist?"

"Oh, sure."

"And wouldn't you have a greater variety, more choice and a more interesting menu?"

"Of course."

"Then what's the point in repetitious one-meal cycles each week?"

"To encourage monotony and to keep meals from being attractive."

Carolyn shook her head as though she expected such an incomprehensible answer and was resigned to it.

"I can see that you deliberately add insult to injury, and by choice. But I can't see why you make it so tough on yourself when you admit you can get the same result by choosing more pleasant means."

I had been waiting for this question. Carolyn was touching one of the root causes responsible for the failure of most weight-reduction schemes. And the single most difficult problem to remedy.

"The key word is choice. To offer an alcoholic a choice of the kind and amount of liquor is obviously self-defeating. For him to stay sober his only choice is not to drink alcohol, which is no choice. To a compulsive overeater, the choice of when, what and how much to eat amounts to the same thing. Freedom to choose his food is precisely what he is incapable of doing because of his compulsion. Therefore, the more attractive and varied his reducing diet is, the worse trouble he gets into. Once I understood this, the solution was simple. Restrict the choice in all matters pertaining to food. The only criteria are medical: i.e., weight control and good nutrition."

"But food is a great pleasure," she protested. "You haven't left room for any fun."

"That's right. Liquor is a great pleasure for the social drinker. But it's poison for the alcoholic. And to an alarming degree, food is a poison to compulsive eaters. We abuse the pleasure and spoil the fun by ruining our health and distorting our looks."

"But aren't you carrying the analogy too far? Food is a necessity. Alcohol is not even important when you get down to it."

"Exactly. Immensely attractive reducing diets make the mistake of adding sensual importance and esthetic interest to necessity in food consumption. But what if the consumer damages himself with the sustenance because he can't choose to eat food any more rationally than an alcoholic can choose to drink liquor? With the alcoholic, the solution is simple: no choice to drink at all. With the glutton, it's not so simple. So you come as close to no choice as health will allow. Therefore, repetitive cycle eating is designed to make meals dull, monotonous, unappetizing and uninteresting. And it pretty well removes the element of choice of amount, time, type and variety of consumption. Here's Cycle IV..."

	BREAKFAST	LUNCH	DINNER
Monday	½ grapefruit Coffee, tea or water	3 oz. cottage cheese, Coffee, tea or water	3 oz. lean broiled steak 3 celery sticks, 1 carrot, Coffee, tea or water
Tuesday	"	"	"
Wednesday	"	"	"
Thursday	"	"	"
Friday	"	"	"
Saturday	"	"	"
Sunday	Liquid diet all day		

A funny thing happened to me on the way to Cycle IV. A friend of mine got into time trouble scoring the music for a TV horse opera and asked me to help out. I drove over to collect the assignment. As we talked it over, his wife served us coffee and placed a plateful of chocolate brownies on the table. I never even knew what hit me. All I remember was talking the job over with Sidney for about fifteen minutes. When I got up to go the plate was empty.

Sidney absently reached for a brownie and upon discovering an empty plate sang out:

"Esther! How about putting some brownies out? Very funny sticking us with an empty plate. Very funny."

Esther stalked in with blood in her eye.

"How did you manage to inhale sixteen brownies without help, Sidney? Look at you growing another pot. Herb's getting to be like a rail. You ought to follow his example. And no more brownies for you. Would you like some, Herb?"

I shook my head, wishing that it would fall off my shoulders. Sidney showed his mettle as a staunch friend and poised man of the world. Shuffling the music sheets, he garbled something unintelligible while he tactfully assisted me to the door. As I left, he merely reiterated how grateful he was that I was helping him out with the time jam he was in.

On the way back, I thought about the Blackout Binge I had just had. The temptation to stop at the nearest place selling food, cooked or raw, was terrific. But appalled as I was, my theory had included the possibility of such an episode as had just happened. I needed a little time to review and understand it. First off, I admitted that like people all over, I was neither perfect nor impossible. And secondly, there was nothing in the Scriptures or anyplace else that required me to follow one piece of idiocy with another. Nor was I compelled to conclude that this binge meant final and total failure. Nor did it condemn all future attempts to that famous road paved with good intentions.

My new theory accepted that an occasional binge might be expected, but that such a binge could be confined to an isolated event and didn't signify a hopeless return to bite, bite, jaw, jaw, swallow, swallow and bloat, bloat. All recriminations had to be seen as a homemade devil's tool fabricating stale reasons why it was impossible to resume the new cycle of eating.

Carolyn listened to my confession that evening without interrupting. When I finished she said, "From what you told me, you're really likely to go banana split every so often."

"Right. But more rare than often. And a one-shot split at that."

"How do you know?"

"Because of what I understand about myself now. First off, on the subject of food, I'm crazy. That means I can't play games that someday in the future, everything will change and I'll be like everybody else. The fact is that I'll never be able to judge how much is enough or too much, or even what tastes good, because nobody eats sixteen brownies at a clip because they taste good. Secondly, I won't be falling for every fancy new reducing diet that claims miracles. Thirdly, the scale will be the final judge. I know damn well that if I refuse to weigh myself regularly, it's because I want to play ostrich by eating like a pig. But iron-clad, gilt-edged security that there won't be more than an occasional minor goof or even a major goof, I don't have. One hundred percent doesn't exist in this life. As long as I don't behave as though a passing mistake is an unredeemable catastrophe, I'm safe. Using a simple louse-up as an excuse to turn myself into a disaster area is part of food craziness. And knowing *that* means I can accept that a crazy symptom will show up once in a while without going completely crazy."

"But are you going to be on this cycle way of eating all your life?"

"Until something better shows up. I popped by the doctor's office after raping the brownies and told him what I'm doing. He said it was perfectly sound medically."

"But what happens when you finally get down to your right weight? You can't go on losing forever. Won't you have to stop the cycle business?"

"No. I'll just switch to scale cycle: That means adding two eggs and a slice of buttered toast to breakfast and half a baked potato and salad dressing to dinner. The cycle pattern will remain the same. The proof will be in the daily scale readout. If there's any gain or loss it will show up. Then I can adjust the cycle accordingly."

Carolyn looked sad for a moment.

"I know this sounds ridiculous. But I could almost cry about all the fun and adventure in food you have to miss. And that I can't cook mad recipes for you once in a while."

"Look at it this way, honey. Some people wear glasses, others need hearing aids and there's a big bunch of people who are color blind. I have to wear a muzzle, so to speak. That's a small price to pay compared with the moral bankruptcy of constant failure. And who knows? Maybe they'll invent a skinny pill some day."

I turned over the last three cycles.

Cycle V:

	BREAKFAST	LUNCH	DINNER
Monday	½ grapefruit Coffee, tea or water	3 oz. cottage cheese, Coffee, tea or water	Broiled 3 oz. hamburger Salad without dressing, Coffee, tea or water
Tuesday	"	"	"
Wednesday	"	"	"
Thursday	"	"	"
Friday	"	"	"
Saturday	"	"	"
Sunday	Liquid diet all day		

DIARY OF A FOOD ADDICT

Cycle VI:

	BREAKFAST	LUNCH	DINNER
Monday	½ grapefruit Coffee, tea or water	3 oz. cottage cheese, Coffee, tea or water	Slice of ham Cooked spinach Coffee, tea or water
Tuesday	"	"	"
Wednesday	"	"	"
Thursday	"	"	"
Friday	"	"	"
Saturday	"	"	"
Sunday	Liquid diet all day		

Cycle VII:

	BREAKFAST	LUNCH	DINNER
Monday	½ grapefruit Coffee, tea or water	3 oz. cottage cheese, Coffee, tea or water	6 cooked shrimp, Salad without dress-ing, Coffee, tea or water
Tuesday	"	"	"
Wednesday	"	"	"
Thursday	"	"	"
Friday	"	"	"
Saturday	"	"	"
Sunday	Liquid diet all day		

After I completed the seven cycles, I began over again. By the time I made it through Cycle IV the second time around, the scale read right.

Then I added two eggs and a slice of toast for breakfast, some salad dressing and a baked potato and butter for dinner. But I used the scale every day rather than weekly. By adjusting my cyclical eating pattern to hold my weight fairly steady, I went through two more cycles without varying more than two or three pounds.

Carolyn had gotten used to the routine and with the passing of time completely lost her self-consciousness at mealtime. She ate what and when she pleased without reference to me. Of course, since she didn't have a problem, her weight remained steady and she continued to look like a sylph.

One night we had some friends in for dinner, one of whom had the fat plague. After dinner he asked me what kind of diet I was following. When I explained that the burgeoning number of reducing diets had the fatal flaw of emphasizing food to people who required quite the opposite, he got riled. And when I explained how cyclic eating did the job, his temper flared even more.

But I was hardly the one to be smug or superior. I figured that at least five years of successful weight control would be necessary before I could begin to make claims backed up with solid proof. I answered his barbed questions as objectively as I could, being especially careful not to respond to his provocations.

I was in for two surprises that night. The first one came when everybody joined in the discussion rather heatedly. Most of the people didn't even have marginal difficulties, let alone compulsive eating patterns. But they had strong opinions about cause and cure. Their voices were raised like clenched fists and they could have been discussing politics or religion judging by their manner.

The second surprise came during a lull in the noise. The fat one spoke up.

"There are a few things I've been dying to ask you. What is the most important reason for losing weight?"

"There are two important reasons. Health and looks. There are plenty of other good reasons, but those two, in my opinion, are paramount. And of the two, health is number one. You cut your life span by a hell of a percentage by being overweight. And you risk a bunch of miserable diseases on the way to the grave."

"But if this weight thing is just so you can stay healthy longer in order to die of old age, it won't work," he objected. "I mean, look at the cigarette thing. People don't stop smoking even though they know they can get cancer from it. So I can't get too excited about all those terrible stories about how sick I may get some day in the future. Your whole number falls apart unless you come up with better reasons."

"You're right. It's the present that counts. There's something ridiculous about saying 'Starve your todays, live more tomorrows.' But it is the present, the todays, the everydays, that are the torment of the fat person. He thinks he's worse than other people because his looks are distorted. A person can hide almost anything he's deeply ashamed of unless it's fat. There he is, naked: convicted of greed, indulgence, weakness, sloth. A self-made caricature. He waddles when he might be walking. He gasps when he could be breathing. He cringes wondering what others wonder about his sex life. He endures the humiliation of euphemisms such as 'portly' or 'ample' or 'outsize' when shopping for clothes and never permits himself a whim for a style or a witty design. He can't suddenly hop or skip or jump for the sheer hell of it. And the ordinary things such as a theater seat, an automobile ride, a place on a park bench, bending to smell a rose, become extraordinary events requiring lavish exhibitions of nonchalance. The only peace he knows is loneliness. Yet he needs someone, some human contact. He finds it by dialing information and asking for his own number again and again."

"That's right," the fat man said softly, "that's the way it is. I call nighttime radio talk shows. That's the way it really is, man. The only time you feel equal is when nobody can see you."

After we'd gone to bed, I lay awake longer than usual. I wondered whether Carolyn or any other slender person really understood the fat problem. After a while, I decided it didn't really matter. I was too drowsy to speculate any further and ready to drop off when the night light flickered and went out, its life spent. Just as it did I heard a familiar whisper, an old echo.

"Time for me to go, Fatso. Open up, let me out." It was Skinny.

I answered silently, "Oh, no you don't. Not on your life. I'm still a fat man. So I'm keeping three extra pounds around just to make sure of you. Because I'm just not that sure of me."

As I held on to my wife, I uttered a quiet prayer:

Give us this day our daily bread. But, dear God, please make mine a half chicken breast without skin.